British Depth Studies c.500–1100 (Anglo-Saxon and Norman Britain)

Anthem Press
An imprint of Wimbledon Publishing Company
www.anthempress.com

This edition first published in UK and USA 2018
by ANTHEM PRESS
75–76 Blackfriars Road, London SE1 8HA, UK
or PO Box 9779, London SW19 7ZG, UK
and
244 Madison Ave #116, New York, NY 10016, USA

British Library Cataloguing-in-Publication Data
A catalogue record for this book is available from the British Library.

ISBN-13: 978-1-78308-808-9 (Pbk)
ISBN-10: 1-78308-808-7 (Pbk)

This title is also available as an e-book.

To all our students, who have helped in more ways than they can know.

Contents

Who Is This Book for?

This book is designed for students and teachers preparing for the new GCSE 'Anglo-Saxon and Norman England' British Depth Study components of the Edexcel and AQA examination boards.

Each chapter follows the same structure and form, namely:

- A list of the key issues relevant to the theme of the chapter and directly addressing the Edexcel and AQA specifications
- A timeline
- A brief overview of the contents of the chapter
- A detailed discussion of each key issue, frequently employing primary material
- Question and/or a series of questions/tasks at the end of each key issue designed to test reader's understanding
- Series of questions in the style adopted by Edexcel and AQA at the end of each chapter
- Suggestions for key websites useful for extension work and consolidation in the final section of each chapter.

At the end of the book is a detailed glossary and useful index. (Words shown in bold upon their first use indicate that they are featured in the glossary.)

This book includes many carefully chosen primary sources, a large number of which have never before been made available to students at this level. These serve to provide a richer, fuller flavour of the period than other textbooks. These sources are 'folded' organically into the narrative, so that history is presented in its most attractive format – as a story.

1 THE CREATION OF ENGLAND

Key Issues

Timeline

800 BC: Beginning of Iron Age (BC stands for 'Before Christ')

AD 43: Arrival of the Romans (AD stands for 'Anno Domini', which is a Latin phrase meaning 'in the year of our Lord', referring to the year of Christ's birth)

407: Collapse of the Roman Empire; beginning of invasions by Angles, Saxons and Jutes

597: Arrival of Augustine

793: Viking attack on the monastery of Lindisfarne

871–899: King Alfred

878: Battle of Edington and Treaty of Wedmore

937: Battle of Brunanburh

991: Danegeld first levied

Overview

The island that by the tenth century was to become known as 'Engla land' owed much of its character to separate phases of invasion and settlement that occurred over the course of the previous one thousand years. The indigenous (native) tribes of the Iron Age experienced first the arrival of the Romans (c.50–407) followed by the Angles, Saxons and Jutes (400–c.700) and then the Vikings and Normans (700–c.1000). Territory in the far north – the country we know today as Scotland – and Ireland experienced only occasional incursions from these newcomers, and these areas therefore developed differently from England. A key influence from around the sixth century (in this instance, in Ireland as well as in England) was the gradual spread of **Christianity**, a consequence of the work of missionaries such as Augustine (d c.604). As Christianity spread and began to be adopted by English kings, it developed its own organization known as the **church**. (See Chapter 7.) Thus, by the time of the Norman Conquest of the mid-eleventh century, England already had a rich heritage and a complex and fascinating history.

1) What do we know of England before the coming of the Romans?

The history of England before the Roman invasions from the mid-first century BC is difficult to determine. No written records exist from this time, and therefore our knowledge of this period is derived from archaeological evidence and other more substantial physical remains. For instance, the survival of hill forts demonstrates the existence of many warring tribes. Artefacts such as bronze axes, gold beads and torcs (neck-rings) were sometimes placed together and buried in collections known as **hoards**, perhaps with the intention of recovery at a later date or as a ritual offering to one of the many **pagan** gods. Taken as a whole, evidence of this sort demonstrates that England was a vibrant and wealthy society, and in turn explains why it was attractive to the Romans.

Questions

1) Study Source A. What can you learn from this map about England before the coming of the Romans? Explain your answer.

2) Study Sources B, C and D. What do these sources suggest about the organization and lifestyles of the tribes that produced them?

Source A. Map showing late Iron Age England.

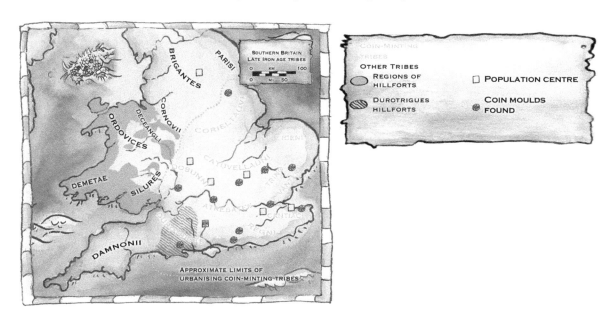

Source B. The Great Torc, a neck-ring mostly made of gold alloyed with a small part of silver. It was found in 1950 at Snettisham in Norfolk, East Anglia. It had been buried with a bracelet and a coin, which helped date the torc to around 75 BC.

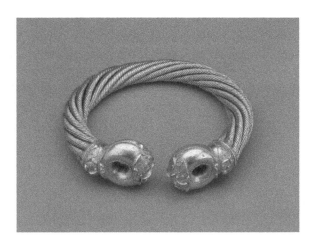

Source C. Maiden Castle, Dorset. A fortified settlement built some time before the coming of the Romans.

Source D. The Burton Hoard, Wrexham. Thirteenth to mid-twelfth century BC. It includes two bronze plastaves (axes), one bronze chisel, one gold torc, one gold twisted-wire bracelet, gold necklace pendant, four gold beads, three gold rings and one pottery vessel fragment.

Our first eyewitness accounts of the peoples of Britain are provided by the Romans. Julius Caesar undertook two invasions in 55 and 54 BC, initiating a period of Roman influence and rule that was to last until AD 407. Recent research has shown that Britain was more heavily Romanized than was thought. Across Wales and the north there was heavy Roman investment and town planning. Yet the Romans found their northern border consistently threatened, and thus in AD c.142 they built between the rivers Forth and the Clyde a line of turf defences, the Antonine Wall. Unable to hold this line from attacks by tribes in the far north, they withdrew some forty years later behind the much more robust Hadrian's Wall, erected from stone between the River Tyne and Solway Firth after the visit of the Emperor Hadrian.

Questions

1) Study Sources A–E. What can you learn about the inhabitants of Britain from these sources during the Roman occupation? Explain your answer with reference to the sources.

2) Explain why a historian may be cautious about fully trusting B, D and E.

Source A. Map showing the Roman occupation of Britain.

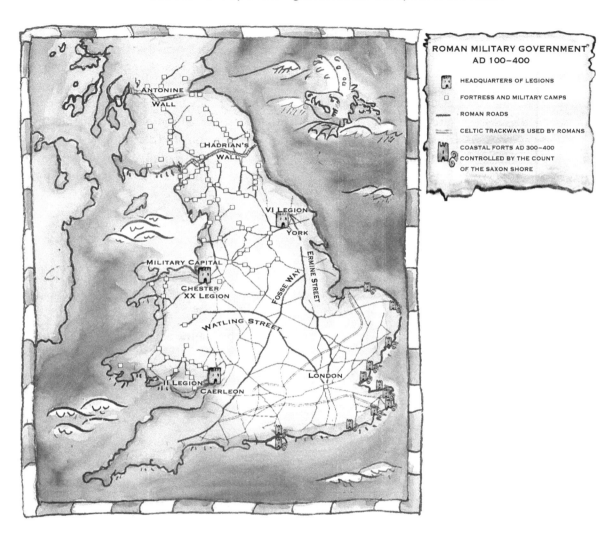

Source B. Julius Caesar, from the *Gallic Wars. The campaign against Britain of 54 BC.*

The interior of Britain is inhabited by those of whom it is traditionally said that they were born in the island itself, while in the maritime portions [areas next to the sea] live those who had passed over from the country of the Belgae [the region of modern Normandy and Belgium] to plunder and make war. Almost all of them are named after the names of the tribes from which they originated. They went over to Britain [from Gaul] to wage war, but stayed there and began to cultivate the land. Most of the inland inhabitants do not plant grain, but live on milk and flesh, and are clad with [animal] skins. All the inhabitants dye themselves with **woad**, which causes a bluish colour that gives them a more terrible appearance in battle. They wear their hair long and have every part of their body shaved except their head and upper lip.

Source C. A fifteenth-century copy of Ptolemy's map of Britain, (originally drawn in the 2nd century AD), followed by a modern version. Both maps show the names and locations of the native tribes.

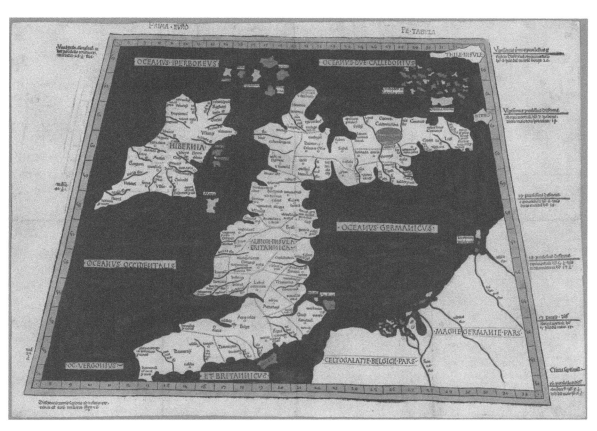

PEOPLES OF
SOUTHERN BRITAIN
c. 150
BASED ON PTOLEMY'S MAP

0   KM   100

0   MI   50

Source D. A description of native resistance to the Romans in AD 61 on the Isle of Anglesey from *Roman History* by Cassius Dio (d. AD 235).

> On the shore stood the opposing army with its dense array of armed warriors, while between the ranks dashed women, in black attire like the Furies [goddesses of justice and revenge], with hair tangled and messy, waving sticks. All around, the Druids [pagan priests], lifting up their hands to heaven, and pouring forth dreadful [intimidating] chants, scared our soldiers by the unfamiliar sight.

Source E. From *Agricola*, by Tacitus, written AD 98c. (Boudicca was queen of the Iceni people of Eastern England and led a major uprising against occupying Roman forces in AD 60 or 61.)

> Under the leadership of Boudicca [queen of Icini in Norfolk area, eastern England], a woman of kingly descent (for they admit no distinction of sex in their royal successions), they all had risen in arms. They had fallen upon our troops, which were scattered on garrison duty, stormed the forts, and burst into the colony itself, the head-quarters, as they thought, of tyranny. In their rage and their triumph, they spared no variety of a barbarian's cruelty. Had not Paulinus [the Roman governor of Britain c.AD 60] heard of the outbreak and brought prompt aid, Britain would have been lost. In one successful battle, he brought it back to its former obedience, though many, troubled by the conscious guilt of rebellion and by particular dread of Paulinus, still kept to their arms.

2) Who were the Anglo-Saxons and what was their impact on the existing population of England?

After the collapse of the Roman Empire, around 407 warlike tribes known as Angles, Saxons and Jutes invaded from their continental homelands in what is now northern Germany and Denmark. (This is the period in which the Romano-British resistance fighter King Arthur apparently fought. However, the historical basis for the existence of any such figure has long been debated.) Nineteenth-century historians argued that these Germanic and Scandinavian invaders settled along ethnic lines in distinct regions, such as Kent (Jutes), Middlesex and Sussex (mid- and south-Saxons), and East Anglia (eastern Angles). This interpretation drew mainly upon the work of the eighth-century chronicler Bede (673–735). The island the invaders populated later came to be known as 'Englaland', which means 'land of the Angles'.

Questions

1) Study Source A. Use Source A and your own knowledge to outline what you understand by the names 'Angles', 'Saxons' and 'Jutes'.

2) Study Source B. What does Gildas say about the nature of the Saxon invaders?

3) Study Sources B and C. To what extent does Bede seemed to have based his account on the writing of Gildas? Explain your answer.

Source A. Map showing the settlement routes of Angles, Saxons and Jutes.

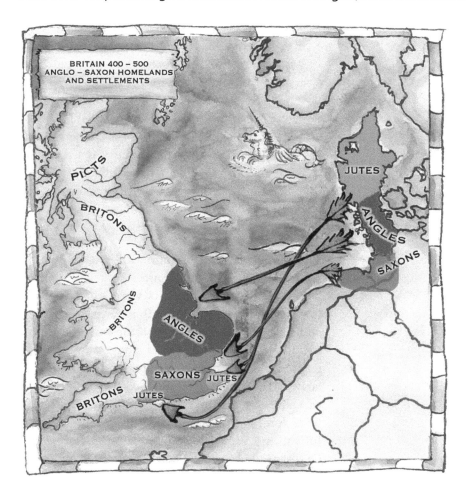

Source B. Gildas, *The Ruin of Britain*. Gildas was a sixth-century monk who described the arrival of the German invaders.

> Gurthrigern [Vortigern], the British king, and his advisers, were so blinded, that, in trying to protect their country [from attacks by the Scots], they sealed its doom by inviting in among them (like wolves into the sheep-fold), the fierce and godless Saxons to repel the invasions of the northern nations

[the Scots]. [When the Saxons arrived] the fire of vengeance spread from sea to sea and did not cease, until, destroying the neighbouring towns and lands, it reached the other side of the island, and dipped its red and savage tongue in the western ocean. [Those who survived the onslaught] were taken in the mountains and murdered in great numbers; others, constrained by famine, came and yielded themselves to be slaves for ever to their foes, running the risk of being instantly slain, which truly was the greatest favour that could be offered them: some others went into exile.

Source C. Bede, *Ecclesiastical History of the English People*, c.730.

In AD 449 the Angles or Saxons came to Britain at the invitation of King Vortigern [a fifth century warlord and leader of the Britons] and were granted lands in the eastern part of the island on condition that they protect the country. Nevertheless, their real intention was to subdue it whereupon a larger fleet quickly came over with a great body of warriors, which proved to be an invincible army. These newcomers were from the three most formidable races of Germany, the Saxons, Angles and the Jutes. The first commanders are said to have been the two brothers Hengist and Horsa. In a short time, swarms of the aforesaid nations [the Angles, Saxons and Jutes] came over into the island, and these foreigners began to increase so much, that they became a source of terror to the natives who had invited them.

The traditional interpretation offered by Bede is now understood as too simplistic. Historians dispute the scale of immigration. Some scholars believe that the immigrants were small military elites who seized control through battle, while others argue that they came in large numbers and settled by agreement with the existing occupants. Saxon burials often included shields and spears, suggesting a warrior culture which might explain their success in eventually dominating the south, while the similarly warlike Angles established themselves mainly in the Midlands, the east and the north. Yet the same burials show that the various settlers were trading and living together. Many of the immigrants were indeed Jutish, and especially Saxon and Anglian, but some Scandinavian and Germanic tribes had been long settled under Roman rule while others were immigrants from other parts of the continent, such as Frisians from modern Holland, Franks from northern France and Swabians from southern Germany. These immigrants did not settle exclusively in ethnically segregated areas of the country but intermingled with each other and the native inhabitants. In reality, we know very little about events in the century after the collapse of the Roman Empire because of an absence of reliable sources and archaeological artefacts. Hence this period has often been dubbed the 'Dark Ages'.

Questions

1) Study Source A. How far does this source support the current interpretation offered by historians about the colonization of Britain by the Angles, Saxons and Jutes after the collapse of the Roman Empire? Explain your answer.

2) Study Source B. How convincing is this interpretation about the impact of the various invaders of Britain? Explain your answer using Interpretation B and your contextual knowledge.

Source A. Map showing the settlement of Angles, Saxons and Jutes c.600.

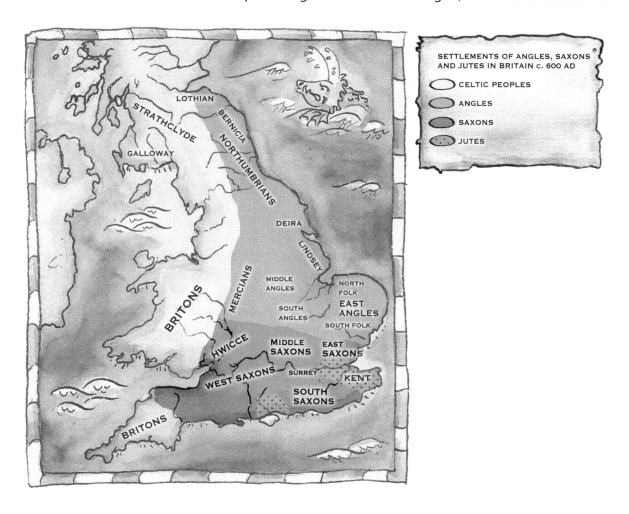

Source B. Simon James, BBC History website 2011.

> Contrary to the traditional idea that Britain originally possessed a 'Celtic' uniformity, which first Roman, then Saxon and other invaders disrupted, in reality Britain has always been home to multiple peoples.

3) What were the origins of England?

After the fall of the Roman Empire early in the fifth century, Britain comprised a patchwork of various tribes occupying localized territories. These territories were loosely based around the old Roman network of administration centred on towns, now decaying. Relationships between the different tribal groups were fluid and unpredictable, but over the next two centuries they repeatedly amalgamated with, or conquered, their neighbours, with the effect that smaller tribes were absorbed into larger political units and territories each recognizing its own king until seven major territories emerged, collectively known as the **Heptarchy**: East Anglia, Mercia, Northumbria, Wessex, Essex, Kent and Sussex. Each of these territories had its own warrior kings. The fortunes of these emerging kingdoms ebbed and flowed. Northumbria was dominant in the seventh century, Mercia in the eighth, then Wessex in the ninth.

This process of amalgamation is well illustrated through the example of Mercia, which originated as a group of tribes of West Angles based in what is now the north-west Midlands, but then grew through the conquest and amalgamation of the Middle Angles, and of lesser kingdoms such as Lindsey in modern Lincolnshire. By the end of the seventh century Mercia extended across most of central England. It also controlled other kingdoms and tribal areas around its boundaries as either satellite or buffer states to protect its borders, including Wessex and Kent. Crucially, it also controlled the trading centre of London, which provided access to luxury goods and the profits from trade with the Continent.

Mercian leaders had cemented their control by either marrying into the ruling elites of these buffer states or acquiring sizeable tracts of land there. Mercia also developed a rudimentary system of taxing the territories subject to its authority, based on an assessment of the number of 'hides' each comprised, known as the Tribal **Hidage**. A **hide** was a unit of taxation, based on an area of cultivated land roughly equivalent to perhaps 120 acres, though recent research has indicated that it in fact had a very variable extent on the ground. The extensive kingdom of East Anglia was rated at 30,000 hides. In contrast, the smaller territory belonging to one of the last of the old tribes, known as the Hicca, which occupied an area on the south-east frontier of Mercia around what is now Hitchin in north Hertfordshire and south Bedfordshire, was assessed at a mere 300 hides. This determined how much taxation the Hicca paid (whether in money, foodstuffs or military aid) when the Mercians demanded it.

By the end of the eighth century Mercia, led by King Offa (r. 757–96) was at the peak of its power. It was defended on its western boundary with Wales by a massive earthwork (known as a dyke) running from north to south constructed under Offa (though recent archaeological investigation suggests that some sections were built by his predecessors). Protection around the rest of its territory was provided by **burhs** (fortified settlements). However, under the leadership of King Alfred (see pp. 25–26), Wessex emerged as a military force in the early ninth century, challenging Mercia's control over its dependent territories and increasing its influence in western areas of Mercia. Mercia was then further weakened by the cumulative effect of Danish raids, until the arrival of the Great Viking Army in 865 brought much of Mercia under Danish rule. Later the kings of Wessex extended their control over the remaining **Anglo-Saxon** territories and the Danish settlement of the **Danelaw**, so that by the tenth century they governed a country that came to be known from that time as Engla-land, England.

Questions

1) Study Source A. Use Source A and your own knowledge to explain what you understand by the 'Heptarchy'.

2) Study Sources B, C and D. Use Sources B, C and D and your own knowledge to explain the emergence of Mercia by the end of the eighth century. Use each of the following in your answer:

   - satellite/buffer states
   - intermarriage
   - Tribal Hidage
   - Offa's Dyke
   - Burhs

Source A. Anglo-Saxon England in c.800.

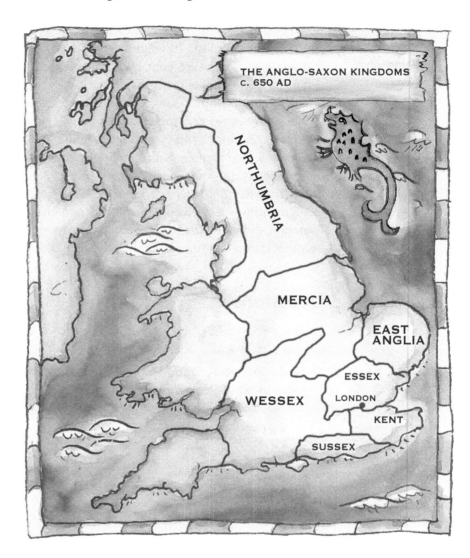

Source B. A map showing the location of Offa's Dyke.

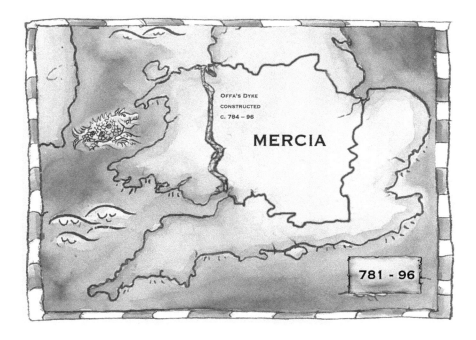

Source C. A section of Offa's Dyke.

Source D. The burh 'wall' at Wallingford in Oxfordshire.

4) Who were the Vikings and why did they invade England?

Between the eighth and eleventh centuries a further phase of invasion and settlement occurred, this time undertaken by adventurers – latterly known as Vikings – from Scandinavia, mainly Denmark and Norway. Norwegian Vikings probably attacked Scotland and Ireland, and Danish Vikings – the 'Danes' – more southerly areas. Unlike the majority of the English population who had by this time converted to Christianity, the Vikings worshipped many gods including Odin, the god of war, music and poetry.

The initial motivation for Viking attacks upon England is in part explained by the lure of valuable items of silver and gold – principally chalices (drinking cups), plates, bowls and crucifixes concentrated in the recently established, and poorly protected, Christian churches and monasteries. The attack in 793 on the monastery of Lindisfarne off the coast of Northumberland is usually seen as the beginning of the Viking age. Over the course of the ninth and tenth centuries, population expansion and dynastic quarrels in Scandinavia triggered further invasions.

The Vikings had developed advanced seafaring abilities based upon the fast, versatile, robust, yet light, longship. Their raiding and exploration took them as far west as modern North America and as far east as European Russia. The origins of the duchy of Normandy (from 'Normannia', the land of men from the north) in northern France are to be found in an early tenth-century settlement of Vikings around the town of Rouen and the River Seine. The leader of these first settlers was Rollo (r. 911–27), William the Conqueror's great-great-great-grandfather.

Questions

1) Use Source A and your own knowledge to explain why Vikings invaded England from the eighth century.

2) Study Sources B, C and D. How far do Sources B and C explain what is shown in D? Explain your answer.

Source A. Map showing Viking attacks on Britain.

Source B. A Viking ship being excavated in a burial mound at Gokstad, Norway, in 1880.

Source C. An modern replica of a Viking ship.

Source D. Map showing areas of north-east Europe settled/raided by the Vikings.

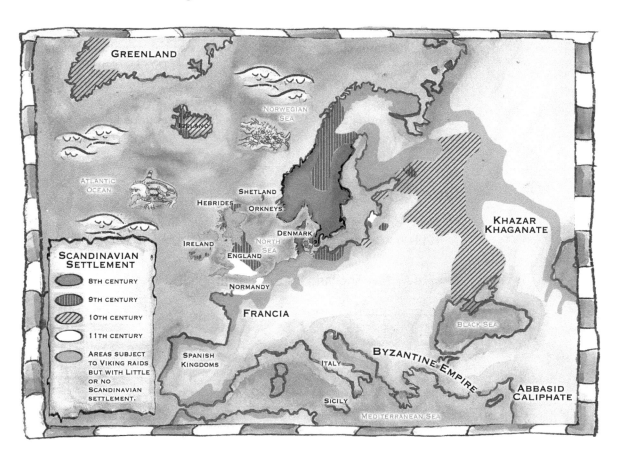

5) What was the Danelaw?

The initial Viking incursions during the early ninth century were no more than military raids, but later attempts by Vikings to settle in the British Isles culminated in the arrival of a large Danish army, known as the Great Army, in East Anglia in 865. The pagan Danes defeated in battle and killed the devout Christian Edmund, king of East Anglia (r. c.855–69), and over the next 10 years they conquered the Anglo-Saxon kingdom of Northumbria and most of the territory belonging to the kingdom of Mercia, including London. Only Kent and Wessex resisted under Alfred, the Anglo- Saxon leader of Wessex (871–99).

King Alfred of Wessex eventually defeated the Danish leader Guthrum in battle at Edington in 878. The Treaty of Wedmore later in the same year brought an end to this phase of hostilities. The key terms of this treaty were that Guthrum agreed to convert to Christianity, and the Danes established their control over the territory roughly north and east of a line drawn from London to Chester, and south of another drawn on the latitude of the River

Tyne. The territory in which the Danes established their control became known as the 'Danelaw'.

The Danes strengthened their rule of the Danelaw by upgrading the fortifications of the old Mercian burhs of Derby, Leicester, Lincoln, Nottingham and Stamford, and establishing them as important administrative and trading centres. York (Norse = *Jorvik*) became a major Danish centre in the north. Archaeological evidence suggests that these places had been largely administrative centres in the Anglian kingdom of Mercia, but from the mid-ninth century under Danish influence they developed important industrial and commercial functions.

Question

1) Study Sources A and B. Use these sources and your own knowledge to explain what you understand by the term 'Danelaw'.

Source A. Map showing the movements of the Great Army and Guthrum.

Source B. Map showing England in the ninth century.

---

6) What was the impact of the Viking invasion on the existing population of England?

Source Investigation: The Viking Raids – what was their impact and what was the English response? Study Sources A–D.

1) What can you learn from these sources about the character and impact of the Viking raids?

2) What can you learn from these sources about how the English responded to these raids?

3) Study Sources A and D. Explain why a historian might be cautious about trusting these sources?

Source A. Symeon of Durham, *History of the Kings.* **Symeon (d. c.1129) was a monk in Durham, writing in the early twelfth century.**

793. In this year the pagans from the northern regions came with a naval force to Britain like stinging hornets and spread on all sides like fearful wolves, robbed, tore and slaughtered not only beasts of burden, sheep and oxen, but even priests and companies of monks and nuns. And they came to the church of Lindisfarne, laid everything waste with grievous plundering, trampled the holy places with polluted steps, dug up the altars and seized all the treasures of the holy church.

Source B. Extracts from the *Anglo-Saxon Chronicle.* **The** *Chronicle* **was first begun at the end of the ninth century. It is a contemporary record of events, written by monks in England.**

991. In this year Ipswich was ravaged and very soon afterwards **Ealdorman** Brihtnoth was killed at Maldon. And in that year it was determined that tribute [money] should first be paid to the Danish men because of the great terror they were causing along the coast. The first payment was 10,000 pounds. **Archbishop** Sigeric first advised that course.

1001. Here in this year there was great hostility in the land of the English race through the raiding ship-army; and they raided and burned almost everywhere. And then Hampshire came against them and fought with them. And there Aethelweard, the king's high-reeve, was killed, and Leofric of Whitchurch and Leofwine, the king's high-reeve, and Wulfhere, the bishop's thegn and eighty-one men in all. And there were many more of the Danish killed, though they had possession of the place of slaughter.

1011. In this year the king and his councillors sent to the [Viking] army and asked for peace, and promised them tribute [money] and provisions on condition that they should cease their ravaging. [The Vikings overran much territory because] they were never offered tribute in time nor [were they] fought against.

Source C. Extract from a royal charter (a grant) of King Ethelred the Unready dated 1005.

In our days we suffer the fires of war and the plundering of our riches, and from the cruel actions of barbarian enemies engaged in ravaging our country and from the many sufferings inflicted on us by pagan races threatening us with extermination we perceive that we live in perilous times.

Source D. The *Knutsdrapa***, a poem about King Cnut (r. 1016–35) by Ottar the Black. Ottar seems to have entered Cnut's service. The poem was probably written around the time of the events it describes – attacks upon England by Cnut in 1015–16.**

Young leader, you made the English fall close by the [River] Tees. The deep dyke flowed over the bodies of the Northumbrians. You broke the raven's sleep, waker of battle. Bold son of Swein, you led an attack at Sherston, farther to the south. There I know that you took [English] lives, breaker of the peace of shields. [King] Edmund's noble offspring met with deadly wounds.

Historians in the 1960s modified the unflattering view of Vikings as marauding invaders by observing that much of the bad press associated with Vikings was written by Anglo-Saxon monks – those who felt most keenly the impact of Viking raids. These historians also point to archaeological evidence suggesting that substantial numbers of Vikings settled as farmers in many places that they raided, and that they frequently blended in with the indigenous (native) population through intermarriage. Assimilation, they argued, occurred gradually through intermarriage, intermingling and the conversion of Danes to Christianity. Indeed, some large stone crosses incorporate Christian and pagan imagery, representing perhaps an early stage in the Viking conversion to Christianity and indicating a blending of cultures. Moreover, according to this 'peaceful' Viking school of thought, place-name evidence has also been misconstrued. Whilst it is true that place names of modern English villages in the Danelaw reflect Viking arrival, either through the presence of Scandinavian personal names or through the use of the Norse words for village (*–by*) and hamlet (*–thorpe*), it is of significance that the language as a whole remained English.

This view has in turn been challenged. Recent historians emphasize that when Viking raids resumed in the 980s a number of defeats were inflicted upon the English, and in response King Ethelred ordered in 1002 all male Danes living in England be killed – an occasion known as the St Brice's Day Massacre. This event seems to indicate that even a century after their first arrival the 'Danes' were still seen as a distinct group to the 'English' – powerful evidence to diminish the 'peaceful' Viking thesis.

Questions

1) Study Sources A–D. For each of these sources explain which of the various interpretations of the impact of the Vikings it best supports. (Consider whether a single source may permit more than more interpretation.)

2) Why do you think interpretations about the impact of immigration keep changing?

3) Which interpretation about the impact of the Vikings do you find most convincing? Explain your answer.

Source A. Map showing the distribution of Scandinavian place names.

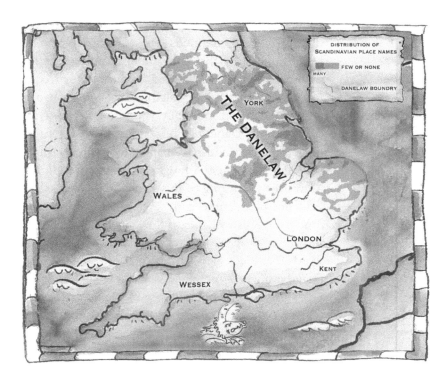

Source B. Vale of York Hoard, including Viking silver coins and ingots in a Carolingian cup plundered from a monastery. (The Carolingians were a European dynasty that existed in the ninth century.) The hoard contains coins relating to Islam and to the pre-Christian religion of the Vikings, as well as to Christianity. The hoard was probably buried for safety by a wealthy Viking leader during the unrest that followed the conquest of the Viking kingdom of Northumbria in AD 927 by the Anglo-Saxon king Athelstan, (r. 924–39).

Source C. The *Anglo-Saxon Chronicle,* for the year 1002. The Chronicle was first begun at the end of the ninth century. It is a contemporary record of events, written by monks in England.

> And in that year the king ordered to be slain all the Danish men who were in England – this was done on St Brice's day – because the king had been informed that they would treacherously deprive him, and then all his councillors, of life, and possess this kingdom afterwards.

Source D. The chronicle of John of Wallingford. This account comes from a chronicle written by an anonymous author in the early thirteenth century.

> They [the Danes] had also either seized, or prepared to seize, all the best towns in the island, and caused much trouble to the natives of the land they interfered with the married women, and persuaded the daughters even of the nobles to be their concubines (mistresses). For these and other like causes there arose many quarrels and wars in the realm. Eventually, from the constant influx of their countrymen, they had so increased in numbers and strength, that they paid but little respect to the king so that at last he was so provoked by the numerous complaints arising from their insolence, that he gave them all up to the English to be dealt with as they might think fit. They spared neither sex nor age, destroying together with them those women of their own nation who had consented to intermix with the Danes, and the children who had sprung from that foul adultery. Some women had their breasts cut off; others were buried alive in the ground; while the children were dashed to pieces against posts and stones.

7) What was King Alfred's contribution to the emergence of England?

Alfred became king of Wessex in 871, when Wessex's resistance to attacks by the Danes was desperate. Indeed, Alfred was reduced to hiding in the Somerset marshes in Athelney. Here, according to the popular legend that first emerges in the twelfth century, Alfred's host asked him to watch over some cakes that were baking in the oven, but the king allowed them to burn because he was so preoccupied with the task he faced. Alfred regrouped successfully and in 878 defeated a Viking force led by Guthrum at the Battle of Edington. While the formation of the Danelaw enabled the Danes to consolidate their hold over this territory, Alfred used the peace to create a chain of fortified burhs (fortified towns and forts) across his kingdom of Wessex to protect against future Viking aggression. Alfred is the only English king to be known as 'the Great'. (This epithet was not applied until the sixteenth century.)

The stress of responding to the presence of a great Viking army after 865 forged significant changes to the administration of Wessex, which many historians have regarded as decisive steps towards the nation state of England: the implementation of effective administrative change; the establishment of new law codes (published in Old English); and the creation of a fleet of ships to defend the coast and tidal rivers. Above all, this emerging sense of a nation was provided with common points of cultural reference by Alfred, who himself translated key historical works into English in order to encourage God's support in the struggle against the Vikings. These included the *Ecclesiastical History of the English People*, by the monk Bede (d. 735), which, as we have seen, told of the arrival of the Angles and Saxons and of their conversion to Christianity.

Hostilities were renewed in the early tenth century, complicated this time by further Viking raids in the north and dynastic quarrels within the ruling elites of the Danelaw and Wessex. Yet the main theme to note in this period is the subjugation (bringing under control) of the Danelaw territories by Alfred's descendants, the kings of Wessex, led by Edward the Elder (r. 899–924), his sister Æthelflæd and Alfred's grandson Athelstan (r. 927–39).

As Wessex gradually conquered the Danelaw region, it united all the kingdoms under one ruler. Athelstan is generally regarded as the first king of all England because of his decisive defeat of Viking forces in 937, at the Battle of Brunanburh.

Questions

1) Study Source A. Use Source A and your own knowledge to describe how King Alfred responded to the main Viking invasion.

2) Explain how Alfred's resistance to the Vikings appears to have contributed to the emergence of England.

Source A. Map showing the burhs established by King Alfred.

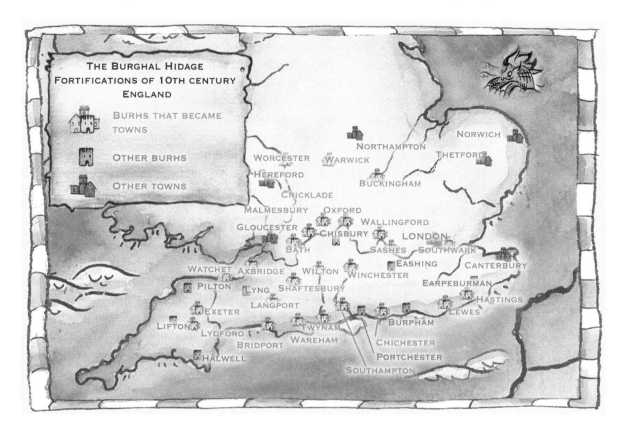

8) How did the concept of English kingship emerge?

i) The origins of kingship

The growth in the size of political territories from the fifth century was also associated with the rise of the office of kingship. The earlier and smaller tribal units may well have been led by either a group of elders or chiefs who were not obviously much wealthier than other members of the tribe, judging from the archaeological remains of burial sites. Yet the gradual process of tribal units coming together (through conquest and intermarriage) into larger ones encouraged a shift to a more hierarchical leadership, as the existing elites or chiefs were displaced by an overlord – an individual, recognized by all as having a legitimate claim to be their leader. This was the most powerful man in the territory, who took the title of king.

The word 'king' comes from the Old English 'cyning'. The exact role of the earliest kings cannot be known for certain, but it appears to have varied. Kingship was shared in some of the early kingdoms, and kings were usually selected by a council of leading men. It was possible for an individual to be selected as king on the basis of his personal qualities, such as Penda (r. 628–55), who became king of Mercia not through the lineage of his family but

27

through his genius as a war leader, although this did not save him from being killed in battle. Penda was the last great pagan Anglo-Saxon king.

As the size of kingdoms grew in the fifth and sixth centuries, so too did the military and economic resources upon which their leaders could draw and in this in turn further defined the concept of kingship. The high status and wealth of some the earliest kings of the early Anglo-Saxon period have been dramatically revealed by the archaeological findings at Sutton Hoo (Suffolk), where an early seventh-century burial ship revealed valuable and ornate jewellery and a superb warrior's helmet, which had probably belonged to Raedwald, c.599–c.624, ruler of the important kingdom of East Anglia.

The concept of kingship was advertised and consolidated by crafting an image of the king on coins. Every time a coin changed hands, it thus brought to mind the individual who claimed authority over all others. Unsurprisingly, English kings asserted control over the manufacture ('minting') and use of coins. It is a claim that can be traced far back into the Anglo-Saxon period and it was enforced brutally. King Athelstan (r. 924–27) ordered that 'if a minter be convicted of striking bad money, the hand with which he was guilty shall be cut off and set up on the mint-smithy'. Eventually, uniformity throughout England was achieved in 973 by King Edgar (r. 959–75) after he decreed in a law code that 'one coinage is to be current throughout all the king's dominion, and no man is to refuse it'. His ruling appears to have been successful; archaeological evidence shows that the king's coin was the only one allowed to circulate. It is certain that silver pennies, the only actual coins, were minted by the million.

Questions

1) Study Sources A and B. What can you learn about early kingship from these sources? Explain your answer.

2) Study Sources A–D. Use these sources and your own knowledge to explain how the concept of English kingship emerged in the period from the fifth century.

Source A. Burial chamber of the Sutton Hoo ship-burial 1, England. Reconstruction in the Sutton Hoo Exhibition Hall. This is perhaps the burial chamber of Raedwald, king of East Anglia (r. c.560–c.620).

Source B. An extract from *Beowulf*, a poem composed in Anglo-Saxon (Old English) at some point between the seventh and the tenth centuries. It may have been recited in the feasting halls of Anglo-Saxon lords and kings. This extract describes the burial of Scyld, king of the Danish.

After [the reign of] Scef came [that of] Scyld, the son of Scef, a prince strong in warfare, wise in counsel, generous in giving treasure. When Scyld grew old and weak, and the time drew near that he was to sleep his last sleep, he bade them carry him to the seashore. Thither his people carried him, with grief in their hearts, and laid him in the lap of a warship with treasures of gold and ornaments, with battle-axes, bills [a weapon composed of a pole with a hook shaped blade on its end] and spears, and chain armour; and on his breast they laid rich offerings of jewels and precious stones. A golden flag was laid over his head, and thereupon they unfurled the sails [of the ship] and let the wind bear the ship where it would over the sea.

Source C. A reconstruction of the warrior's helmet found at Sutton Hoo in 'Mound 1', probably belonging to Raedwald (r. c.560–c.620).

Source D. A coin minted during the reign of King Edgar (r.959–75). It shows him draped and wearing a diadem (an ornamental headband worn by monarchs).

ii) The duty of kings

The emergence of larger political units containing more territory and bigger populations also resulted in a change to the ways in which they were ruled. Leaders were required to provide protection and justice to their people, which they did through imposing their personal authority and laws. This meant travelling around the territory continually. However, rulers also needed to establish a social and political organization to provide stability and order across their expanded territories, not just to uphold their authority across them through fighting and visiting in person. From the late seventh century all kings were Christian, and it was part of their duty to promote Christian religion through support for monasteries and by personal example, though the king had to exercise authority over the church. (See Chapter 7). Trade and markets also had to be protected and encouraged. Finally, the stresses of the Viking invasions created a desire for leadership.

By the late ninth century a clear understanding of the role of a king had emerged, usually as the head of a dominant and wealthy dynasty in which his sons or brothers succeeded him to the throne: the basis of modern kingship.

Questions

1) What were the key features of kingship by the late ninth century?

2) Explain why kingship had emerged in recognizable form by the late ninth century.

iii) The coronation ceremony

The authority of a new king was formalized by a consecration ceremony presided over by the church, known as a **coronation**. A special consecration of King Edgar (r. 959–75) towards the end of his reign in 973 set the pattern for all new coronations thereafter and highlighted the key functions of the king of the recently created kingdom of England. In front of the **bishops** the king took a threefold oath: to preserve the peace of the church and the Christian people; to prohibit looting and crime; to maintain justice. The king was then anointed with holy oil, usually by the archbishop of Canterbury. After that the king was presented with a sword with which to defend the church and to protect the weak, a crown was placed upon his head and finally he was presented with an orb and sceptre (a rod), the former representing Christ's supremacy over the world and the latter indicating the king's authority over all other laymen. The nature of the ceremony thus elevated the king's power above that of all other men. In short, for all to see, a king was God's chosen deputy, though there was as yet no 'divine right of kings'. Early medieval kings knew that they would have to work hard to maintain their authority and power. This explains the haste with which Harold had himself crowned in 1066, within hours of the death of Edward the Confessor. He did not want a rival claimant to the English throne to get this essential seal of approval.

Question

1) Study Source A. To what extent does this scene of the crowning of Edward the Confessor confirm your knowledge about the key details of the coronation ceremony?

Source A. An illustration from the mid-thirteenth century *Life of Edward the Confessor*.

9) How did English kings govern in the eleventh century?

i) The monarchy and the church (see Chapter 7 for further details on the church)

Much of the British Isles had converted to Christianity gradually after the arrival of Augustine in 597 and his foundation of Canterbury cathedral. Churches began to be built, many of the more important housing the shrine (tomb) of a saint. The spread of Christian belief as the dominant religion was accompanied by the creation of an administrative structure to parallel the civil administration, led by two archbishops (established at Canterbury and York, the latter founded in 735) and a number of bishops. Each bishop and archbishop was responsible for running the church over a clearly defined territory, called a **diocese**. The bishop operated from a major church within the diocese, known as a cathedral. These territories, the location of the bishop's seat and even the names of the dioceses changed a good deal during the ninth and tenth centuries, but they had settled by the eve of the Conquest of 1066 into 16 dioceses of very different sizes. The dioceses of York and Lincoln were the largest, dominating northern England, and that of Rochester the smallest. The government of the church by bishops is known as episcopacy.

By the eleventh century it had become common practice for the monarch to take the initiative in appointing bishops and **abbots** (the leaders of monasteries), as opposed to the **clergy** of the various churches making this choice. This ability to appoint the chief ministers of the church – known as ecclesiastical patronage – was important from the king's point of view, because such men were major, wealthy lords in their own right, and the king would want to know that such figures were men loyal to him and would be helpful to him in the running of the kingdom. Abbots and bishops were also important because they would need to organize amongst their communities or flocks prayers for the king and kingdom, which in a religious age was considered crucial to success. Ecclesiastical patronage also significantly increased the king's power because it enabled him to reward followers by appointing them to these posts. The bishops had to tread a fine line between supporting their king, managing the clergy within their diocese, and demonstrating loyalty to the pope in Rome, who was the head of the whole of the Western church.

Questions

1) Explain how the monarchy enhanced its power by its relationship with the church.

2) Study Source A. Use your own knowledge and the details in this source to describe the administrative organization of the church.

3) What can you lean about the Christianization of England from Source B?

Source A. Map showing dioceses in existence between 850 and 1035.

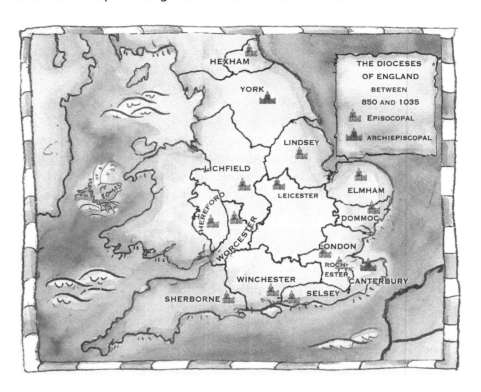

Source B. Map showing the location of the burial sites of Christian saints in England prior to 1066.

ii) The authority of kings

Kings were great landowners in their own right. The lands and estates held by the king were distributed throughout the country, and known as **Ancient Demesne**. This was the 'personal' estate of the king, in the sense that it passed from king to king in succession, and its purpose was to support the king's household and the expenses incurred by him through the process of governance.

Yet the kingdom needed occasionally to raise extra cash to fund exceptional public expenditure, such as raising an army to defend England or to invade other territories. In 991, a national tax was raised to buy peace from Danes, dubbed the **Danegeld**, which proved so effective that it was refined into a system of national taxation whenever exceptional funding was needed. (As we have seen, the amount of money paid in tax was based on the number of hides assessed for each community and county. See p. 12). Kings also benefited from revenues drawn from other sources, such as taxes on trade (customs duties, though not levied systematically until the late thirteenth century) and, increasingly, from fines paid by those found guilty of breaking the law. (See p. 51.)

The king was head of the army and whatever naval forces he could muster. The king did not possess a standing army (i.e. an army that was uniformed, paid, trained and available to call out from barracks at a time of emergency), and there was no royal navy, but he had the means to call out a national force in times of emergency. By 1066, there were two principal elements in this royal army, an inner band of personal retainers – initially composed of the king's personal bodyguards, the **thegns**, but from the time of Cnut (r. 1016–35) known as **huscarls** – and the **fyrd**, which was the body of locally raised militia. Each community contributed to the fyrd according to an assessment of its hidage. Every five hides had to provide one warrior for the army, so a village rated at ten hides had to find two soldiers for the fyrd and send them to the muster point: they would either be men of the village, or the village would have to pay for mercenaries (hired soldiers).

The huscarls were well armed and effectively equipped. The Bayeux Tapestry, an extraordinary 70-metre-long picture story of the Conquest commissioned in the 1070s by King William's half-brother, Bishop Odo, shows them at the Battle of Hastings as infantrymen clad in mail, wearing conical helmets and wielding double-edged axes and swords. The fyrd were less well equipped in terms of armour. Many carried clubs, axes, scythes and haymaking forks – the paraphernalia associated with a rural workforce – although the spear and the shield remained their basic weapons.

Questions

1) Study Source A. Use Source A and your own knowledge to explain what you understand by the term 'Ancient Demesne'.

2) What can you learn from Source A about the nature and scale of the lands held by Edward the Confessor?

3) Study Source B. Use Source B and your own knowledge to describe the key features of an English army in the eleventh century.

4) Briefly describe the status and authority possessed by eleventh-century English kings.

Source A. Map showing the scale and distribution of the lands of Edward the Confessor in 1066.

LANDS OF
KING EDWARD
1066

DEMESNE

1   15   100

HIDES

Source B. An artistic impression of a scene from the Bayeux Tapestry showing the Anglo-Saxon army of Harold at Hastings fighting the mounted Normans. The Tapestry was commissioned by Bishop Odo, the half-brother of William. It was probably made in England in the early 1070s.

iii) The development of a royal administration

a) The king and his councillors

In order to enact his royal will throughout his territories the king required support and assistance from leading men. Before Cnut's reign the highest-ranking secular royal officials, with the authority of a vice **regent** (in effect, a 'second-in-charge') and nominated by the king, were called ealdormen. Each ealdorman exercised jurisdiction (command) on the king's behalf over a wide swathe of territory, called an **earldom**, and was responsible for acting in the king's name in areas where the king himself could not regularly visit to provide personal rule. When the Danish king Cnut came to the English throne, the Danish name for this position – **earl** – stuck. As other systems of local government developed, the number of ealdormanries or earldoms diminished, so that by the early eleventh century they numbered four: Northumbria, Mercia, East Anglia and Wessex, the last of which was the most dominant by this time.

Next in status to the earl were the thegns, lords of local importance who were prominent in the localities. They were landowners who lived in impressive halls with a fortified entrance and a bell tower. In the **hundred** court (see p. 50) their testimony carried weight, and many of the greater thegns attended the king and took a seat at his table when he travelled through their locality.

Parliament did not exist before the thirteenth century. Instead, the leading members of the aristocracy – the king's sons, bishops, abbots, ealdormen/earls and thegns – met with the king in the great council of the realm, the **witenagemot** (or **witan**), to discuss key matters of state. The body met when and where the king determined. It should be noted that the witan was not the precursor of Parliament – it was a much smaller body. That is, it was the king's council, whereas a larger body, which met customarily three times a year (at Christmas, Easter and Whitsun) formed the assemblies that were the forerunners of Parliament.

In the Anglo-Saxon period, lands and titles did not automatically descend to the eldest son. All of the king's sons were known as '**aetheling**', meaning 'throne worthy', and kingship could just as easily pass from one brother to another as from father to son. Often the succession was uncertain – of the eight kings who reigned between 899–1016 only three inherited the throne uncontested – and it was the duty of the witan to decide who would succeed to the throne, thereby introducing a strong elective element into English kingship. Indeed, the only contemporary account of Harold's election as king in January 1066 states that he 'succeeded to the kingdom as the king granted it to him *and* as he was chosen thereto'.

Questions

1) Study Source A. Use Source A and your own knowledge to describe two features of the witan.

2) Study Source B. Use Source B and your own knowledge to describe two features of an earldom.

Source A. An Anglo-Saxon king meeting with his witenagemot.

Source B. A map of England showing the four earldoms in existence at the start of the eleventh century.

b) Local government

The Danes were hugely influential in reshaping the structure of local government in England. In the early ninth century the area of the southern Danelaw and eastern Mercia was reorganized in a new system, based on the **shire**, the equivalent of the modern county. Each shire was named after its **borough**, hence, for example, Bedfordshire after Bedford and Northamptonshire after Northampton. This system coexisted with earlier territorial arrangements in the kingdom of Wessex, where shires were more loosely organized. Shires continued to emerge during the tenth and eleventh centuries. By the time of Domesday Book in 1086 there were 33 shires, most of them between 600 and 1,600 square miles and recognizable in name, size and location as the counties of modern England.

The shire structure of local administration was one of the means by which the kings of Wessex imposed their will on their enlarged kingdom of England. In particular, the shires had important military functions. The local militia, the fyrd, was raised through the **shire**, and groups of shires had a strategic military role, such as providing a first line of defence against Danish invasions.

The shire system, however, had more than a just a military role. It had an important role in bringing local communities together to maintain the peace; to resolve disputes over land; to undertake major infrastructure works such as defensive fortifications, bridge building and sea reclamations; and to organize taxation. It held a regular court, where juries made up of men of the shire decided the matters that came before it. The king's representative was the **shire reeve**, or **sheriff**, who presided over the court alongside a local earl and a bishop. The shire reeve was responsible to the king for the administration of local finance, the execution of justice and the maintenance of customs by which the shire was governed. In effect, he was the king's chief executive agent in every branch of local government, whose role gradually superseded that of the ealdormen.

Shires were subdivided into territories composed of 100 hides, notionally 10 or 20 villages. Each of these subdivisions was a unit of assessment, appropriately known as a hundred. Each had its own court, which the **freemen** of the hundred were obliged to attend.

Questions

1) Study Source A. Use Source A and your own knowledge to explain what you understand by the term 'shire'.

2) Study Source B. Use Source B and your own knowledge to explain why you understand by the term 'hundred'.

3) Study Source C. How might you explain the pattern of density of population shown in this source?

Source A. A map showing the shires of England in 1066.

Source B. A map showing the territorial divisions known as Hundreds in Somerset.

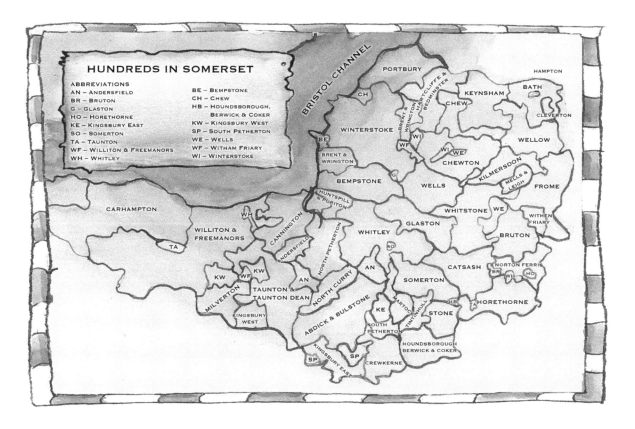

Source C. The population density and distribution in England in 1066.

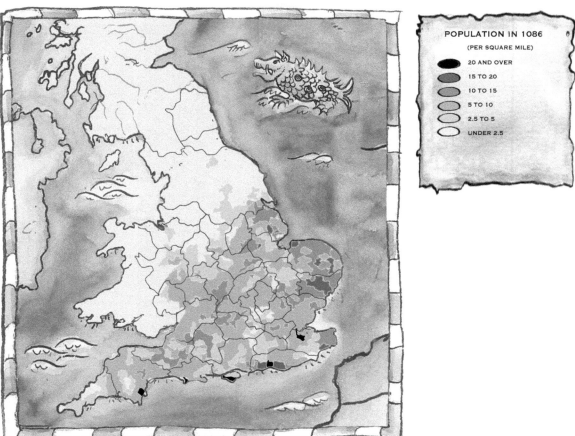

POPULATION IN 1086
(PER SQUARE MILE)

20 AND OVER
15 TO 20
10 TO 15
5 TO 10
2.5 TO 5
UNDER 2.5

c) Writs and charters

Royal instructions were formalized and communicated to sheriffs, bishops, earls and thegns through the use of **writs** and **charters**. Writs carried a brief instruction to a named individual or group of recipients, while charters bestowed a grant of privileges or rights, usually over land. In the eleventh century, the growing use of writs and charters and the importance they acquired in the efficient operation of royal administration led to the development of a royal department of state, the **Chancery**, responsible for maintaining written records. The extraordinary degree of central control acquired by the late Anglo-Saxon monarchy is shown by its supervision of the minting of coins, the dies for which were cut and inspected in London and then sent to each borough, being renewed every few years to maintain the quality of the coinage and maximize profits for the king.

Questions

1) Study Source A. Use Source A and your own knowledge to explain how an Anglo-Saxon king of the late tenth century imposed his authority other than by force. You should use all of the following terms in your answer:

   - ealdormen
   - shire
   - earldoms
   - shire reeve
   - thegn
   - writs
   - charters
   - witenagemot/witan

Source A. A charter of King Aethelwulf of Wessex, dated 843. The charter records the granting of land to his thegn, Aethelmod. Attached to the bottom of the charter are the names of the witnesses. The witnesses would have been deliberately chosen. Their names added authority to the grant and if there was any dispute later then they could be called upon.

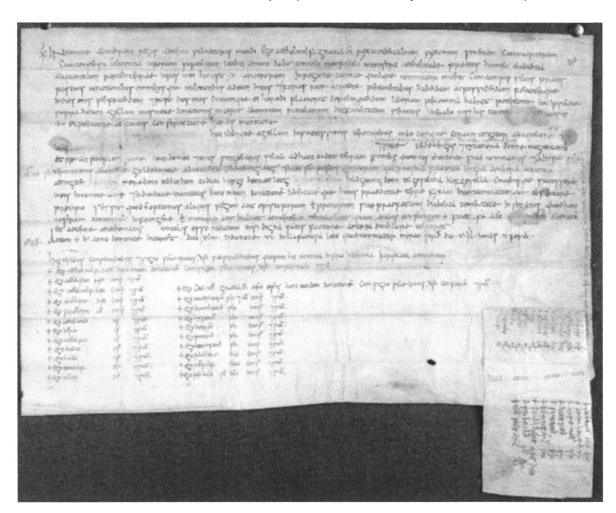

2) 'By the year 1000, Anglo-Saxon England was remarkably well governed'. To what extent do you agree with this statement? Explain your answer.

3) Study Source B. How far do you agree with Carpenter's interpretation of the character of the Anglo-Saxon state? Explain your answer

Source B. David Carpenter. *The Struggle for Mastery* (2003), pp. 61–62.

> The Anglo-Saxon state had three pillars: a powerful sense of Englishness which held king and people together; a kingship high in status and strong in administrative structures; a church, gentry and nobility integrated within the king's government of the realm.

10) Exam practice and online resources
Questions in the style of Edexcel

a) 4 marks per question

i) Describe two features of the hide.

ii) Describe two features of the coronation ceremony experienced by early medieval English kings.

iii) Describe two features of the royal army.

iv) Describe two features of a shire.

b) 12 marks

Explain why England had emerged as recognizable state by the early tenth century. You may use the following in your answer:

The impact of the Vikings
The leadership of King Alfred

You must also use information of your own.

c) 16 marks

'The greater part of the authority of the early medieval Crown was derived from its relationship with the Church'. How far do you agree? You may use the following in your answer:

- bishops and abbots
- the coronation ceremony

You must also use information of your own.

Questions in the style of AQA

a) 8 marks

i) Study Source A. How convincing is this interpretation of the impact of the Vikings upon England in the eighth century? Explain your answer using Interpretation A and your contextual knowledge.

Source A. From a nineteenth century children's book published in 1922, *Erling the Bold* by R. M. Ballantyne. Chapter 5

> Skarpedin, a Danish viking, noted for his daring, cruelty, and success, had taken it into his head to visit the neighbourhood of Horlingdal, and repay in kind a visit which he had received in Denmark the previous summer from a party of norsemen, on which occasion his crops had been burned, his cattle slaughtered, and his lands 'harried' [pillaged], while he chanced to be absent from home. It must be observed that this deed of the northmen was not deemed unusually wicked. It was their custom, and the custom also of their enemies, to go out every summer [by sea] to plunder and ravage the coasts of Denmark, Sweden, Britain, and France, carrying off all the booty they could lay hold of, and as many prisoners as they wanted or could obtain. Then, returning home, they made slaves or 'thralls' of their prisoners, often married the women, and spent the winter in the enjoyment of their plunder.

b) 8 marks per question

i) Explain the importance of the Viking raids for the development of England.

ii) Explain the importance of the coronation ceremony for the authority of English kings.

c) 8 marks per question

i) Write an account of the ways in medieval kings imposed their authority.

ii) Write an account of what you understand by 'the church' in this early medieval period.

iii) Write an account of Alfred the Great's contribution to the emergence of England.

Online Resources

Basic summary of the period of rule by Anglo-Saxon kings https://www.royal.uk/anglo-saxon-kings.

Useful timeline giving the key events relating to the Vikings http://jorvik-viking-centre.co.uk/who-were-the-vikings/viking-timeline/.

Sutton Hoo online tour http://www.suttonhoo.org/tour.asp#.

King Alfred and King Alfred's jewel http://www.teachinghistory100.org/objects/about_the_object/king_alfreds_jewel.

BBC Radio 4 In Our Time. Melvyn Bragg and guests discuss King Alfred http://www.bbc.co.uk/programmes/p003k9gm#in=collection:p01dh5yg.

2 LIFE UNDER THE NORMANS

Key Issues

Timeline

616–618: King Aethelberht of Kent issues royal law code

1085: Domesday Book commissioned by William the Conqueror

1086: Domesday Book completed

1215: Trial by ordeal ended

Overview

We know a good deal about English life under the Normans. The vast majority of people (90 per cent) were peasants who lived on the land and earned a living from agriculture. Towns and trade were growing but still relatively unimportant. County towns were well established as centres of government and defence, and a system of law was already in place throughout the country. A careful study of law codes, some of which were in existence before 1066, shows how wrongdoers were identified and punished, and so provides evidence for how society was regulated. The great survey of land that was undertaken 1085–86 and compiled in Domesday Book records a wealth of minor local details, such as the existence of **parish** churches and the value of the watermill. Above all, it reveals who 'held' land (see p. 63) at the time of the investigation, and who had 'held' it in 1066, and so identifies the greater and lesser landlords, and how the vast majority of English lords had been replaced by Normans. William I defined the principle that all land was 'held' from the king in return for specified, usually military, services and for a specified taxable value. The lords who held their land directly from the king, the 'tenants-in-chief', in turn granted some of this land to lesser lords, also in return for services. The grant of land established a personal bond of loyalty between the giver and the receiver, which was formalized through an act of **homage** (see p. 63) in which the recipient of land swore an oath of '**fealty**' to the grantor. Thus a hierarchical pyramidal structure existed, known as the 'feudal system'.

1) What were the characteristics of the legal system?

All kings were expected to keep order and to provide justice. At his coronation, after swearing to protect the church and her clergy, the monarch promised to forbid all crimes and to provide judgement according to equity (i.e. fairness) and mercy. The king was thus the font of justice: he clarified, revised and codified laws; he was capable of pronouncing judgement himself in cases; and he was expected to appoint justices and officials to enforce the laws.

From an early period, kings issued law codes setting out what acts were considered crimes and what punishments should be issued. The earliest surviving law code was issued by King Aethelberht of Kent in 616 or 618. In issuing his law code, Aethelberht was emulating the kings of the Bible and the Roman emperors, who were seen as model rulers. The law codes were applied in the localities by a system of shire and hundred courts, each of which was a public occasion where the majesty of the king was demonstrated through his representatives who presided over the court.

Each shire held a court which met twice a year, presided over by the sheriff and attended by important landowners. It dealt with cases of theft, violence and land disputes. Each hundred (a territorial division of the shire) also held its own court. These seem to have met once a month, often in the open and usually at a prominent local landmark, and were presided over by the reeve. With no police force or Crown Prosecution Service, cases of wrongdoing were 'pushed' to court by local communities who were held responsible for maintaining law and order through an arrangement known as '**tithings**'.

Within each hundred, the entire male population aged over 12 years old was organized into small groups of men, of 10 or 12 in number. These groups were called tithings, and each tithing was responsible for law and order in its small area. Thus, a tithing would apprehend any of its members who committed a crime, and it was responsible for seeking out any fugitive from justice by raising the 'hue and cry'. This meant shouting, blowing a horn or having the church bells rung. The entire community was then required to respond in an effort to catch the criminal. Members of the tithing were obliged to attend a court presided over by the local lord at which they presented the offender(s) and saw that they were punished. The most serious offences were tried in the shire courts. Anyone who did not attend a court was declared an '**outlaw**', meaning that they could be killed by anyone without the offender receiving punishment.

Anyone charged with a crime and who protested his innocence was able to call forward others of his choosing – oath-helpers or compurgators – to support his plea. If this proved impossible or inconclusive, and denial was still maintained, then the accused would be forced to undergo a 'trial by ordeal': God would determine whether he was guilty. Before 1066 there were two forms of trial by ordeal. Trial by fire obliged the accused to pick up a red-hot iron or to retrieve a stone from a cauldron of boiling water. If the wounds of the accused healed within three days, then this was believed to be a sign from God that he was not guilty. Trial by water meant that the accused was tied up and thrown into water that had been blessed by a priest: if innocent, he would sink; if guilty he would be repelled from the holy water, it not receiving a sinner. No doubt the existence of these fierce 'trials' persuaded many to confess.

Punishments meted out to wrongdoers varied over time and according to the crime. Prison was not often used as punishment, and instead sentences involved fines (a rich source of income for the Crown), mutilation or death (usually by hanging). Early Anglo-Saxon kings allowed the victim of a crime, along with members of his family – his 'kindred' – to inflict punishment upon the criminal. If someone was killed, this meant that the dead person's kindred could seek out and kill the murderer, a form of legitimate violence known as the '**blood feud**'. However, later Anglo-Saxon kings recognized that the blood feud encouraged a lack of order and did not provide a means of redress for those victims unwilling or unable to use violence. Instead of the blood feud, therefore, Anglo-Saxon law codes set out a system of compensation for offences, called **wergild** (man-payment). This set a value on a person's life depending on their status. For instance, according to the laws of Ine (King of Wessex r. 688–726), a nobleman's wergild was 1,200 shillings, whilst that of a freeman was 200 shillings. If a man or woman was killed, then the killer's family would have to pay the wergild to the family of the victim. Over time, wergild also came to be used as a system of fines and compensation payments for other offences. For instance, if a woman was raped, then a proportion of her wergild would have to be paid in compensation. Not all crimes were punished solely according to the wergild system. Some serious crimes such as treason carried the death penalty. Regular offenders suffered mutilation, such as having their having their hand cut off or eyes put out.

Much of the system described above persisted for the period covered by this book, though inevitably there were changes. To the existing trials by ordeal, it seems that William the Conqueror added trial by combat. This involved the accused taking on his accuser, and the two would fight using staffs (substantial wooden poles) or hammers. The winner, it was believed, was determined by God's judgement. King William II (r. 1087–1100; also known as William Rufus) eventually banned trial by ordeal – reportedly because 50 men accused of killing his deer had passed the test – although it continued in some use until it was eventually stopped in 1215 following condemnation by the church. Thereafter judgements were made by the use of juries.

Questions

1) Study Source A. Use Source A and your own knowledge to explain what you understand by 'wergild'.

2) Study Sources B, C and D. Explain the circumstances in which these 'trials' might be used.

Source A. From the laws of King Alfred, (r. 871–99).

> 8. If any one carry off a nun from a nunnery, without the king's or the bishop's leave, let him pay a hundred and twenty shillings, half to the king and half to the bishop and the lord of the church [that presides over the nunnery]
>
> 23. If a dog rends or bites a man to death the owner is to pay 6 shillings at the first offence; if he gives it food, he is to pay on a second occasion 12 shillings, on a third 30 shillings.
>
> 26. If anyone with a band of men kills an innocent man [whose value is] two hundred wergild, he who admits the slaying is to pay the wergild and the fine, and each man who was in that expedition is to pay 30 shillings as compensation for being in that band.

Source B. A medieval representation of trial by fire.

Source C. An artist's impression of trial by water.

Source D. A representation of trial by battle, from a royal record made in 1249.

2) What is meant by the 'royal forest'?

The concept of the forest was introduced to England by William the Conqueror. The term 'forest' in the Middle Ages did not refer to an area filled with trees. It referred instead to land that was subject to a specific body of laws, known as forest law. This territory did often consist of thick concentrations of ancient trees, but also contained arable fields, open pastures, villages and even towns. The purpose of bringing land under forest law was to protect the habitat of wild beasts, especially deer and wild boar, so that these animals could be hunted by the Norman kings and their followers. Hunting was important for practising military skills (such as riding and spearing moving targets) and for providing an informal atmosphere in which the king could bond and conduct business with the men of his court. It also provided a forum in which he could demonstrate his prowess as well as his right – indeed his duty – as king to shed blood and to do so publicly.

Areas designated as forest could be large or small: most of western Gloucestershire (the Forest of Dean) was forest, whereas the forest of Windsor covered a small area around the king's land and residence there. There were no forests in Kent, but many in north-west England and in Hampshire. It has been estimated that forest law covered a third of the country, whilst actual physical woodland probably covered little more than 15 per cent of the whole of England.

Question

1) Study Source A. Use Source A and your own knowledge to explain what you understand by 'Forest Law'.

Source A. Map showing the distribution of the royal forest at the beginning of the thirteenth century.

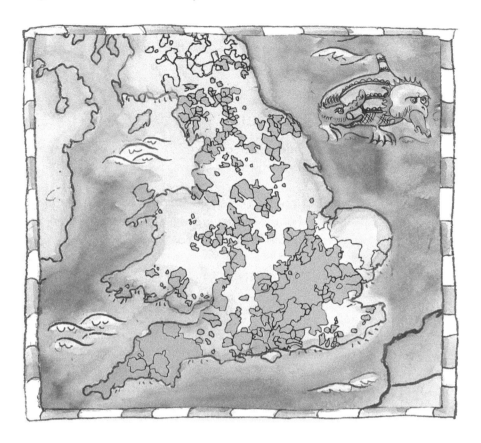

---

3) What was the character of forest law?

Forest law applied to every person within their boundaries. The law stipulated that no person could hunt, fish, build, dig ditches or clear woodland without licence from the king. Inside or outside the forest, kings could also forbid people from hunting the birds that lived around rivers and force local people to build bridges to facilitate the aristocratic sport of hawking. People holding land within the forest were forbidden from creating new areas of arable land and ditching unless they had permission, which was a severe restriction when the population was growing and families were desperate for land. Some people obtained licences at a cost from forest officials, while others went ahead and cleared woods without obtaining a licence on the understanding that they would then receive an **amercement** (fine) in the forest courts. As well as receiving amercements for breaking forest law, wrongdoers could suffer mutilations such as blinding.

A network of royal officers, acting through special courts, was responsible for enforcing forest law. Overseeing the system was the chief justice of the forest, a major office of state to which the king appointed trusted barons. A network of local forest officials policed forest law on the ground. These included wardens,

55

who were men of fairly high status, appointed by the king to oversee particular forests. They carried a hunting horn as a symbol of office. Wardens in turn appointed foresters, who patrolled the forest on the lookout for infringements, carrying a bow as a mark of their office. From time to time specially appointed judges were sent across the kingdom to investigate any breaches of forest law, with the right to amerce anyone who had been caught by the local officials.

Question

1) Study Sources A and B. Use these sources and your own knowledge to explain why forest law was resented.

Source A. The *Anglo-Saxon Chronicle*. The *Chronicle* was first begun at the end of the ninth century. It is a contemporary record of events, written by monks in England.

> The king, William, set up great protection for deer and passed laws so that anyone who killed a hart or a deer should be blinded.

Source B. Adam of Eynsham, *The Life of St Hugh of Lincoln*. This biography of Hugh of Avalon, bishop of Lincoln, 1186–1200, was written by one of his men shortly after the bishop's death. It narrates events that took place during Hugh's rule. Although it is some time after William I, it throws some light on the extent to which forest law was resented.

> The worst abuse in the kingdom of England, under which the country folk groaned, was the tyranny of the foresters. For them violence took the place of law, extortion was praiseworthy, justice was an abomination and innocence a crime. No rank or profession, indeed, to sum up, no one but the king himself was secure from their barbarity, or free from the interference of their tyrannical authority. [It is little wonder that one] forester perished in a very horrible way. He was murdered by certain men whom he had found in the forest and intended to treat in his usual barbarous way. Having cut off his arms and head, his murderers left his truncated body, and severed head and limbs, in three different places along with the medium sized cudgels which they were carrying in the forest, on account of which he had proceeded to maltreat them, as a witness to his cruel and oppressive treatment of the people of the district.

4) What were the main characteristics of towns, villages and industry?

i) Towns

It is estimated that in 1086 there were between 1.5 million and 2.5 million people in England. The total population of Wales, Scotland and Ireland, which are not in Domesday Book, are estimated at less than 2 million. There are some 100 plus towns recorded in Domesday, far fewer than exist today. They were also much smaller. London, the capital, was the largest with an estimated 15,000 people, followed by Lincoln, York and Norwich (c.5,000 each), while most county towns had a population of c.2,000. The biggest towns were responsible for administration and government as well as trade. No more than 10 per cent of the population lived in towns. There were just three towns in the north (Chester, York and Durham), a region of England which was underdeveloped and underpopulated. A large minority of townsfolk were called **burgesses**, men of higher status who ran the borough and who were responsible to the king or to their lord for various military and administrative duties.

The Norman Conquest had a significant impact upon many towns. In most county towns houses were pulled down in the late 1060s to make way for hastily constructed motte and bailey castles, and towns suspected of resistance to William or of Scandinavian sympathies, such as Ipswich, were burnt and plundered. Elsewhere, in places like Old Sarum (Salisbury) and Norwich, new market places and cathedrals were laid out in major projects of urban planning and expansion.

Question

1) Study A. Use Source A and your own knowledge to describe what is known about towns in England at the time of Domesday.

Source A. A map showing towns in England in 1066.

THE LOCATION OF
TOWNS IN ENGLAND
AS REVEALED
IN DOMESDAY

ii) Villages

The Domesday Survey of 1086 (see p. 69) contains information which provides historians with unusually clear insights into the nature of English life. It is not a complete record – for example, the returns for London and parts of the north have not survived – and it was not a census of every person. However, it records townsfolk, agricultural activity, landholders (see below) and values in a standard format across much of the country, which allows comparisons and contrasts to be drawn. From this, we know that 90 per cent of the population lived in the countryside and earned a living from agriculture; that many parts of the south-east had as much land ploughed for crops in 1086 as in 1914; that only 15 per cent of the land surface was still wooded; and that vast areas were still waterlogged marshland, such as the East Anglian fens.

Domesday describes 41 per cent of the people recorded in the Survey as *villani*, 32 per cent as *bordarii* (otherwise known as bordars or cottagers, i.e. people who held little more than a cottage), 14 per cent as freemen and 10 per cent as slaves. The word *villanus* covers a wide range of people, from minor thegns to peasants, but *villani*, bordars and slaves were unfree to varying degrees, which meant they were required to obtain their lord's permission to migrate, to transfer land and to get married. These categories simplify greatly the types of people who existed within a complex and fluid society, but, as a generalization, most freemen and *villani* held small farms of around 15 acres, and the rest held merely a cottage and a smallholding of a couple of acres, or were landless. Freemen could leave their village, and transfer their land to other people, without their lord's permission.

Every peasant belonged to a lord. In practice, peasants were attached to their lord's **manor**. A manor (from the Latin word *manerium*, meaning a residence) was the basic territorial unit of lordship, comprising arable land, pasture, houses, woodland and other economic resources, such as fisheries, mills and mineral rights. At the core of the manor was the manor house, which might be as large as a castle or as small as a house with some agricultural outbuildings, such as barns and stables. The agricultural land belonging to the lord was called the **demesne**, which was used as a home farm to grow crops and rear livestock for the lord's benefit. Other land was allocated to the peasantry for their own benefit, for which they paid rent in cash and kind (such as eggs at Easter), and in manual labour services on the demesne. The peasants often had to grind their grain at the lord's mill. It is popularly assumed that there was one manor to every village, but this was seldom the case. In much of south-east England there were two or three manors to every village, and in the north a single manor might cover a number of villages: the manor of Wakefield (Yorkshire), for example, covered 150 square miles and included the villages of Sandal and Osset as well as Wakefield itself. The majority of villages in modern England are mentioned in Domesday. In 1086, many of these comprised isolated farmsteads or clusters of small hamlets situated around greens, rather than the nucleated villages (nucleated = a village with a large and single centre of settlement) which are so familiar today. Many villages contained just a few families, and the largest totalled around 300 people. At the same time arable land was being organized into regular two- and three-field systems in midland England. Under this system, the land of the peasants and the lord was scattered equally between each field in narrow strips of about half an acre (see Source A, p. 60). These strips were open in the sense that there were no hedges or fences separating them from one another, and farmers identified their own strips through stone markers on the ground. Hence these are known as 'open' fields. All the farmers had to conform to a fixed system of cultivating the land. In the three-field system in one year, all the strips in one field had to be sown with grain during the autumn (wheat or rye), while those in the second field had to be planted with a spring crop (such as barley, oats, peas or beans) and those in the third were not sown at all, but lay unused, or fallow, to allow the soil to recover its nutrients. This continued in sequence over three years, when the rotation started again. A two-field system is similar, based on one sown field and one fallow field each year on a two-year rotation. The fallow – the arable land which was not ploughed at all in a given year – was available to villagers as pasture throughout the year to graze their livestock. Much has been written about the two- and three-field system, but it was probably a fairly new system at the time of Domesday Book and, in any event, it was not found in most parts of

Britain. Cultivated land in much of western and eastern England was never organized into two or three large open fields, but instead its layout was very complicated and irregular. Some land was laid out in patches of small open strips, but much of it lay in either small or large blocks of land enclosed by fences, hedges, ditches or walls. Peasants did not have to cultivate their land on fixed rotations according to the field in which their strip lay, but could do much as they wished. Heaths, woodland, marshes and downs provided grazing pasture for animals.

Agriculture was the biggest sector of the economy. Rural dwellers worked farms of a few acres of land to feed themselves first and foremost, then to sell any surpluses to raise cash to pay their rent. All lords relied upon their estates to provide some food for their household, and monasteries and priests also received grain and some livestock in the form of a payment known as a **tithe**, amounting to one-tenth of the harvest or stock. The main produce was grain – wheat, rye, barley and oats – because this was the most efficient source of calorific intake, and was used to make bread, ale and porridge. Sheep (and goats in northern England) were the most important farm animals, and cattle (mainly oxen) were reared to pull ploughs rather than for their meat or milk. Pigs and poultry were the most important source of meat. The fact that some land was left fallow each year, and that there were few fertilizers, meant that agriculture was not productive by modern standards. Indeed, grain yields were about 5 per cent of modern yields.

Questions

1) Study Source A. Draw a simplified version of this source. Use Source A and your own knowledge to explain what you understand by the three-field system.

2) Study Source B. What tasks are taking place in these images? What other tasks do you know of that medieval villagers would undertake in the course of a year?

Source A. A representation of a village in Midland England with an open three-field system.

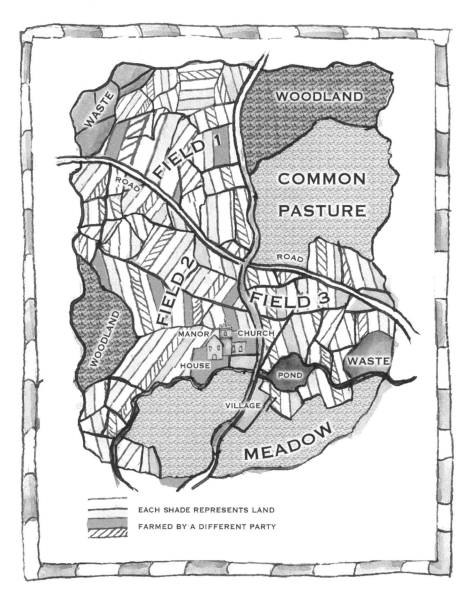

Source B. Illustrations in the Luttrell Psalter (a book containing sacred songs), early fourteenth century.

iii) Industry

There was little industry, and that which existed mainly involved the processing of agricultural goods, such as milling, baking or brewing grain, or working wood and leather into utensils or clothing. Mining for lead and silver (in Derbyshire), ironworking, salt making (from salt springs in Cheshire) and coastal fishing were the other main industrial activities. Historians have calculated that only around 5 per cent of produce was exported. This is reflected in the small number of ports, and the limited references to merchants and ships, in Domesday. English cheese, grain, cloth, wool went mainly to France, the Low Countries (modern-day Holland and Belgium) and Scandinavia, and imports consisted largely of wine, oils, fine cloths, silks and gems – originating from places such as the Low Countries and the Iberian peninsula.

In the 1060s, 44 mints (places in which coins are manufactured) under royal control produced coins to lubricate this trade. Even the smallest farmers were expected to pay part of their rent in cash. In 1086, there was around £40,000 of coin circulating in England, and the smallest coin was a penny. A penny was too large for small and everyday transactions, such as buying a loaf of bread or a jug of ale, so most local trade was based on barter or tokens. There was no Welsh or Scottish currency.

5) What is meant by the term 'feudal society'?

Medieval society was very hierarchical. It assumed the form of a social pyramid with a king at the top, a class of specialized warriors – barons, earls and knights – plus abbots and bishops ('spiritual' warriors) in the next layer, and a peasantry at the base. The relationships between each of the groups in this social pyramid were defined by land because land determined a person's social status and economic wealth. But land was not 'owned' in the modern sense of private property. Instead, land was granted from one person to another, to be 'held' by another in return for personal services of various kinds, loyalty and rent. This social structure, and the holding of land in return for services, is known as the feudal system.

William I established that all land in England was 'held' from the king – not owned – in return for specified services. We know from Domesday Book that in 1086 all the land in England was valued at £73,000, 91 per cent of which was held by either the king or his 300 **tenants-in-chief**. The land held by the king and the royal family was valued at £12,000, around one hundred religious houses (monasteries and nunneries) and bishoprics held £19,000 and 170 tenants-in-chief held £35,000 of land. Very few of the Anglo-Saxon lords who held land in 1066 retained possession of their estates for long, and by 1086 a new aristocracy of mainly Norman lords was established across England. For many, this was the reward for supporting William's venture.

Tenants-in-chief were the most important group of lords in the realm. They were those earls, barons, abbots, priors, bishops and senior knights who held land directly from the king. In this way a tenant-in-chief was 'tied' to the king, performing military service or, in the case of monasteries and bishops, also performing religious services (such as saying prayers for the king and his family, or administering the church) for land. In return, they received protection, justice and could expect the king's support when needed. These landlords in turn granted some of this land to other lords for military or, sometimes, administrative or religious services. All landlords granted some of their land to their peasants, who in this way became 'tied' to a particular lord and were expected to fulfil certain obligations, such as working as agricultural labourers on the lord's demesne land.

Each tenant-in-chief held a number of manors from the king, each one known as a **fief** (or a fee, from the Latin *feudam* = parcel of land). The greatest barons held fiefs in different parts of the country, whereas the fiefs of monasteries and bishoprics were concentrated in the regions in which they were situated. A single fief could be any size, but most comprised a manor of around five hides (= c.600 acres), because this size was considered sufficiently productive to provide the finances to support one fighting knight, that is, to pay for his equipment, horse and support. Most fiefs were known as a **knight's fee**. This system ensured the availability of fighting men to serve the king on request.

Tenants-in-chief granted some of their manors as fiefs to other knights, and to landlords who were not fighting knights (such as heads of smaller monasteries); furthermore, some of these dependent knights and lesser monasteries granted some of their manors to knights of lower status. This process of granting manors as fiefs below the level of tenants-in-chief is known as **sub-infeudation**: all manors were ultimately held from the king, of course, but many lords held their fiefs in a chain of layers below the tenants-in-chief. These layers could become complex, and in the twelfth century, manors were split into smaller manors – much smaller than the standard five hides – and granted to local landlords of low status who held the manor for a half, or a quarter, of a knight's fee.

The knight/landlord who was granted a fief/manor was known as the **vassal** of the superior lord. The grant of land from a superior lord to a vassal also created a strong bond of personal loyalty between the two people. The bond of loyalty was reinforced through the act of homage, which was a ceremony in which the vassal kneeled in front of the lord with clasped hands and swore an oath of 'fealty', that is, faith and loyalty to him. This ceremony symbolized the subjection and obedience of the vassal, which bound them both to serve and protect one another, creating a powerful bond of loyalty and allegiance between lord and vassal.

If a vassal failed to fulfil the terms of the grant – for example, by an act of disloyalty or by failing to fulfil the terms of the military service – then the superior lord could seize the land: this is known as **forfeiture**. His officials would take over the manors and manage them until either the vassal submitted (apologized and made amends) to the lord, whereupon the lands would be restored to the vassal, or the lord decided to grant the land to someone else instead. The threat and the act of forfeiture was a powerful lever for ensuring obedience and a close relationship between lord and vassal.

Many early historians – such as Norman J. Pounds, Allen Brown and V. H. Galbraith – argued that the system described above was introduced by William I. The need to organize an effective military system resulted in the introduction of a new concept of knighthood and knight's fees, in which the grant of a fief formed a bond between land, military service, land and personal loyalty. Lords knew exactly what their military obligations were, and estates and manors were reorganized to rationalize this system. The 'Normanization' of land holding can be viewed as a social revolution. The creation of knights' fees was certainly a clearer and sharper form of social contract than had existed before 1066, but historians now tend to emphasize that William was clarifying an existing system, and that ideas about knighthood, military service and land tenure were refined, developed and codified for a century after 1066. The Normans refined a version of feudal society in England. They did not create it.

Questions

1) Study Source A. Draw your own version of Source A. Complete your diagram by adding these terms in the appropriate location (you may use a term on more than one occasion):

- tenants-in-chief
- grant of land
- knight's fee

2) Study Sources B, C and D. Use these sources and your own knowledge to explain what you understand by the term 'feudalism'. Include the following in your answer:

- vassal
- homage
- forfeiture
- 'holding' of land
- knight's fee
- sub-infeudation

Source A. A diagram showing the feudal system.

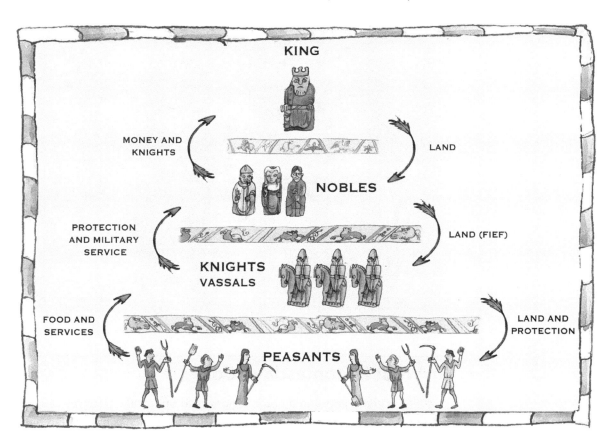

Source B. A writ issued by William, probably in 1072. It is addressed to the Abbot of Evesham.

William, king of the English, to Athelwig, abbot of Evesham, greeting. I order you to summon all those who are subject to your administration and jurisdiction [i.e. under your authority] that they bring me at Clarendon on the Octave of Pentecost [a date: some 50 days after Easter] all the knights they owe me duly equipped. You also on that day shall come to me and bring with you fully equipped those 5 knights which you owe me in respect of your abbacy. Witness Eudo the steward. At Winchester.

Source C. A grant of land by Gilbert, Abbot of Westminster. c.1083.

I Gilbert, the abbot of Westminster, have granted to William Baynard the manor of Tottenham, to be held by him for the whole of his life for the service of one knight on condition that the land reverts to the church on his death.

Source D. A vassal paying homage to his lord with a scribe recording the details of the grant.

6) What is Domesday Book?

In 1086, William appointed commissioners to undertake a survey of land in England. This survey provides details of who 'held' (see p. 63) the land at the time of the investigation and also who 'held' it in 1066, directly prior to the accession of William. A total of 13,418 places are recorded. According to the *Anglo-Saxon Chronicle*, the commissioners conducted their survey so thoroughly that 'not one ox, nor one cow' was left unrecorded. They travelled around the counties of England on routes known as circuits (see p. 68). The manuscript record of this survey became known from the twelfth century as Domesday Book (Book of Judgement) because as a record it was considered unalterable and final: just like the Last Judgement, it could not be appealed.

Questions

1) Study Source A. What seems to have happened to Wulfweard?

2) Study Source A. i) What has happened to the scale of the tax assessment for Crofton? ii) What does this suggest about the impact of the Norman Conquest on Crofton?

3) Study Source A. What can you learn about social structure/organization from this source?

4) Study Source A. What can you learn about economic activity taking place in Crofton?

5) How far do Sources A, B and C support the comment by the *Anglo-Saxon Chronicle* that 'not one ox, nor one cow' was left unrecorded?

Source A. An entry from *Domesday Book* from the shire of Hampshire, the land of Count Alan of Brittany. (TRE stands for 'tempore regis Edwardi', meaning 'at the time of King Edward [the Confessor]'.)

In Titchfield *Hundred*. Count Alan holds Crofton. Wulfweard held it, and could go where he would with this land. TRE it was *assessed* at 7 hides; now at 3 hides less half a **virgate**. There is land for 5 ploughs. To the *demesne* belong 1 plough; and 11 *villeins* and 2 *bordars* with 4½ ploughs. There is a church, and 4 slaves, and a mill rendering [earning] 12s. 6d., and a fishery with 2 salt-pans rendering 100d., and 24 acres of *meadow*, [and] woodland for 5 pigs. TRE it was worth £8; and afterwards 100s., now £4.

Technical terms explained:

Hundred: part of a county that was one hundred hides in size

Hide: a piece of land large enough for one family to live on. It was notionally 120 acres, but it could range in actual size from 40 to 120 acres.

Assessed at 7 hides: these hides are not actual units of land but units of tax assessment (geld).

Virgate: one-quarter of a hide

Demesne: land which only the earl of the lord of the manor used.

Villein: a upper-ranking unfree peasant. Villeins owned land but also had to work on earl's land, the demesne.

Bordar: an unfree peasant who had very little or no land

Meadow: land used for grazing animals and growing hay

Plough: a reference to a team of oxen and one plough

12s. 6d: s = shilling (12 old pence; 5 pence in modern currency); *d* = pence. *£1* = 20s, or 240 pence.

Source B. A map showing the circuits travelled by the Domesday commissioners.

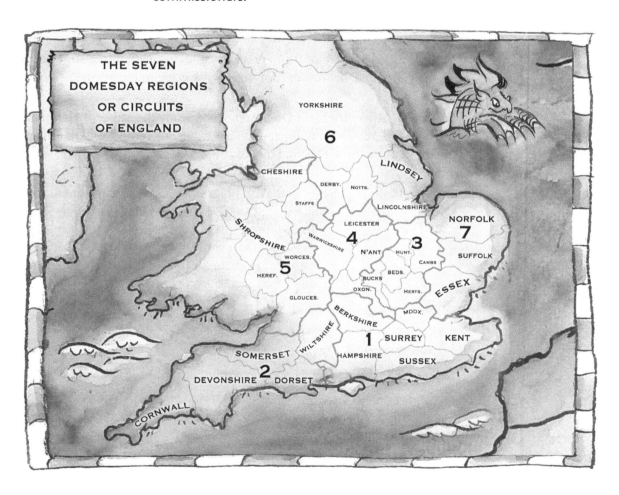

Source C. Map showing the location of places mentioned in Domesday Book.

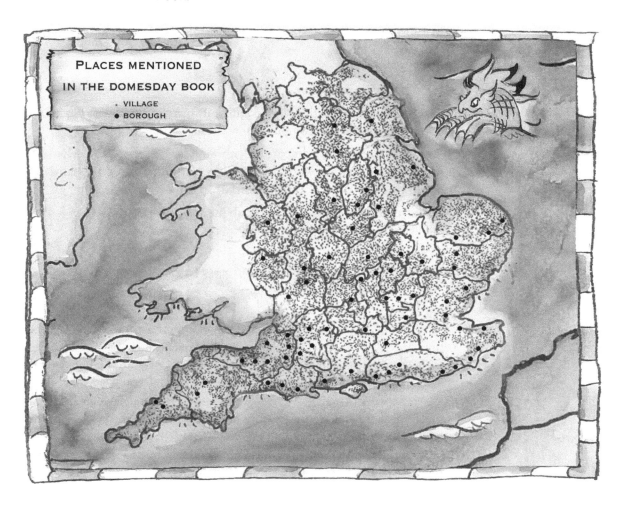

PLACES MENTIONED
IN THE DOMESDAY BOOK
· VILLAGE
● BOROUGH

7) How was Domesday Book compiled?

For the Domesday Survey, the kingdom was divided into seven regional 'circuits', each consisting of about five shires. A group of commissioners was appointed for each circuit. These men then presided over special meetings of the shire courts (see p. 50). Every piece of land in the kingdom was to be accounted for, and every landholder was called before the court to answer a series of questions, with panels of local men acting as jurors to provide evidence.

The commissioners were tasked with finding out who held each piece of land at the time of the survey and who had held it in 1066, together with details of livestock and pasture as well as the land's annual revenue (and how this had changed since the time of the Conquest). The findings from each circuit were written up (in Latin) by scribes working for the commissioners and these documents were then submitted to the king. Amazingly, a single scribe then began the task of writing-up the results into one, authoritative document. The whole process – from William's initial orders to the completion of Domesday Book – took about 12 months: a remarkable testament to the skills and efficiency of the royal officers, commissioners and scribes, as well as the cooperation of the landholders of England.

Questions

1) Study Source A. Use this source and your own knowledge to explain how Domesday Book was compiled.

2) Study Source A and compare it with Source A on p. 67. To what extent does it seem that the commissioners in Hampshire used the same set of questions as those in Cambridgeshire? Explain your answer.

3) What do these sources suggest about the administrative capacity and ability of William's government? Explain your answer.

Source A. *The Ely Inquest*, a contemporary copy of the questions asked by commissioners in Cambridgeshire.

[The commissioners] inquired what the manor was called; who held it at the time of King Edward [the Confessor]; who holds it now; how many hides there are; how many ploughs in demesne (held by the lord) and how many belonging to the men; how many villagers; how many cottagers; how many slaves; how many freemen; how many sokemen; how much woodland; how much meadow; how much pasture; how many mills; how many fisheries; how much had been added to or taken away from the estate; what it used to be worth altogether; what it is worth now; and how much each freeman and sokeman had and has. All this was to be recorded thrice, namely as it was in the time of King Edward [the Confessor], as it was when King William gave it and as it is now. And it was also to be noted whether more could be taken than is now being taken.

Technical terms explained:

Manor: an estate or unit of lordship

Sokeman: freeman who nevertheless had to attend at his lord's court

8) Why was Domesday Book compiled?

William's motives in commissioning Domesday Book have been debated. It used to be thought that Domesday was intended to help the king tax his subjects more thoroughly, but this interpretation has been challenged. Stephen Baxter has pointed out that anyone hoping to use Domesday Book to assess tax liabilities across the kingdom would have a very difficult time because of the way that it is organized. It is not set out village by village (which would have made tax collection easier) but by shire. Each section begins with a table of contents listing the landholders of that shire/county, beginning with the king himself (that is, all the lands managed directly by royal officers on the king's behalf), and then listing all the bishops, abbots, earls and barons who held land from the king in that shire in descending order of status.

In short, the structure of Domesday Book is perfectly designed for easily finding all the landholdings of any particular major landholder. This gave William great power over his barons, because the king could threaten to take away the land of anyone who disobeyed him. This was especially important to William in 1085, Baxter suggests, because at this time he was facing 'the greatest crisis of his life': a rebellion led by his eldest son, Robert, at the same time as a threatened invasion of England by King Cnut of Denmark (see p. 173). William needed to bolster his authority as king and demand the loyalty of his barons.

George Garnett has gone even further in arguing that Domesday Book was intended as an ideological weapon. It was designed first and foremost, he argues, to justify William's claim to be rightful king of England. This was part of a broader campaign by writers at William's court to write a new version of history that showed William as the undisputed successor to Edward the Confessor. As we have seen, for every piece of land, Domesday gave the name of the person who held it on the day that Edward the Confessor died and the name of the person who held it at the time of the 1086 survey. Harold Godwinson is hardly mentioned at all and certainly not as king. William claimed that Edward the Confessor bequeathed England to him, as Garnett argues, 'as if it were a piece of land or a chattel [item], left in a will. In other words, it was William's. The whole kingdom was his, for he was heir to it. Whatever land anyone held in the kingdom was therefore held either directly or intermediately of the king.'

Questions

1) Study Source A. What reason(s) are given in this source for William ordering the Domesday Survey?

2) Study Source B. Use Source B and your own knowledge to explain Stephen Baxter's argument for William commissioning Domesday.

3) Study Source C. How convincing do you find the interpretation of Domesday Book put forward by Garnett? Explain your answer.

Source A. *The Anglo-Saxon Chronicle* (1085). The Chronicle was first begun at the end of the ninth century. It is a contemporary record of events, written by monks in England.

People said and declared for a fact, that Cnut, king of Denmark, son of King Swein, was setting out in this direction and meant to conquer this country with the help of Robert, count of Flanders. When William, king of England, found about this, he went to England with a larger force of mounted men and infantry from France and Brittany than had ever come to this country. Then at Christmas, the king was at Gloucester with his council the king had much thought and very deep discussion with his council about this country – how it was occupied or with what sort of people. Then he sent his men over all England into every shire and had them find out how many hundred hides there were in the shire, or what land and cattle the king himself had in the country, or what dues he ought to have in twelve months from the shire. Also he had a record made of how much land his archbishops had, and his bishops and his abbots and ears – and though I relate it at too great length – what or how much everybody had who was occupying land in England, in land or cattle, and how much money it was worth. So very narrowly did he have it investigated, that there was no single hide nor virgate of land, nor indeed (it is a shame to relate but it seemed no shame to him to do) one ox nor one cow nor one pig which was there left out, and not put down in his record; and all these records were brought afterwards.

Source B. Opening page in Domesday Book for Berkshire beginning with a numbered list of landholders followed by a description of boroughs (towns) starting with Wallingford.

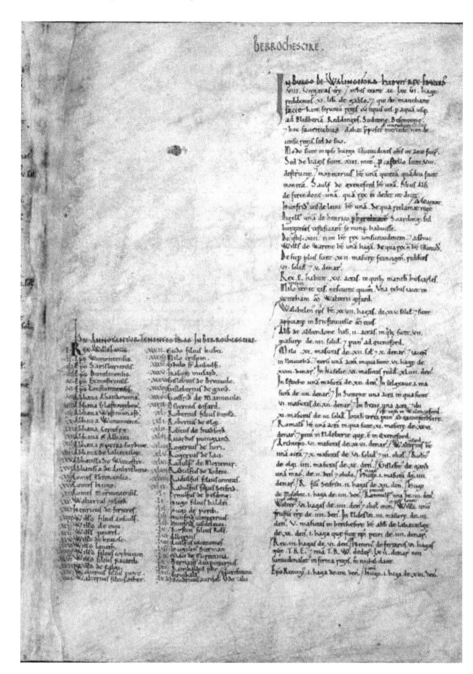

Source C. *Conquered England*, George Garnett, 2007.

Like many totalitarian regimes in the twentieth century, the Normans seem to have realized that control of the past was a prerequisite [an absolute requirement] for mastery of the present, and set about propagating [establishing] an official version of history. Domesday Book represent[s] an attempt to draw a final line under the almost total revolution in both the personnel and the character of aristocratic landholding which had followed the Conquest. [In Domesday Book] Harold is not treated as a king, even a perjured one [a king who broke his oath]; his reign never happened; it was written out of history.

9) Exam practice and online resources

Questions in the style of Edexcel

a) 4 marks per question

i) Describe two features of the 'royal forest'.

ii) Describe two features of Domesday Book.

b) 12 marks

Explain why William I commissioned the Domesday Survey. You may use the following in your answer:

- to help the king tax his subjects more thoroughly
- to enhance the power of the king over his subjects

You must also use information of your own.

c) 16 marks

'By establishing that all land in England was "held" by the king William I significantly entrenched his authority'. How far do you agree? You may use the following in your answer:

- fiefs
- acts of homage

You must also us information of your own.

Questions in the style of AQA

a) 8 marks per question

i) Study Source A. How convincing is this interpretation of the operation of royal justice in England before 1066? Explain your answer using Interpretation B and your contextual knowledge.

Source A. From *Ruling England* by R. Huscroft, 2005.

The operation of the shire and hundred courts, public occasions where authority was exercised on the king's behalf by his agents, mean that royal authority over the lives of ordinary people was being extended, primarily through the operation and application of the law. The hundred court, indeed, with its monthly meetings, must have provided most people with their primary experience of royal government in action.

ii) Study Interpretation B. How convincing is Interpretation B about the Norman legal system? Explain your answer using Interpretation B and your contextual knowledge.

Interpretation B. This is an interpretation of the legal system in Norman times. It depicts a law court and trial by battle. The picture was drawn in 1963 for a children's storybook.

b) 8 marks per question

i) Explain how justice was enforced in territorial divisions known as hundreds.

ii) Explain why the forest law caused resentment.

iii) Explain why William commissioned Domesday Book.

c) 8 marks per question

i) Write an account of the content and purpose(s) of Domesday Book.

ii) Write an account of ordeal by trial.

Online Resources

What did England look like in 1066? Tom Williamson and Mark Bailey from UEA set the scene for the Norman Conquest by discussing the physical landscapes of medieval England. https://www.uea.ac.uk/history/podcasts.

Domesday Book online. http://www.domesdaybook.co.uk/index.html Explore the various tabs.

Various aspects of Domesday Book as presented by The National Archives http://www.nationalarchives.gov.uk/domesday/.

Domesday Book UEA podcast in which Ann Williams introduces some of the complexities of Domesday Book https://www.uea.ac.uk/history/podcasts.

Very much an advanced site, but worth a look once the basics have been mastered. Explore the various tabs on this exhaustive Domesday site http://www.domesdaybook.net/home.

The Luttrell Psalter in high-definition photographs http://www.bl.uk/turning-the-pages/?id=a0f935d0-a678-11db-83e4-0050c2490048&type=book.

BBC Radio 4 In Our Time. Melvyn Bragg and guest discuss Domesday Book http://www.bbc.co.uk/programmes/b040llvb#in=collection:p01dh5yg.

3 THE BACKGROUND TO 1066: WILLIAM THE CONQUEROR, EDWARD THE CONFESSOR AND THE GODWINS

Key Issues

Timeline

1027–28: Birth of William the Conqueror

1036: Edward and his brother Alfred visit England; Alfred is murdered by Godwin.

1043: Accession of Edward

1047: Battle of Val-es-Dunes

1051: Godwins go into exile; Edward (probably) nominates William his successor.

1052: Godwins return from exile

1053: Harold becomes Earl of Wessex.

1057: Death of Edgar the Atheling

1064: Harold at the court of William in Normandy; takes oath of fealty

1065: Tostig goes into exile.

Overview

This chapter introduces the key personalities of William the Conqueror, Edward the Confessor and important members of the Godwin family, especially Godwin, Earl of Wessex, and his son Harold, crowned King Harold II in January 1066.

1) Who were the Normans?

The Normans kings governed England between 1066 and 1154, beginning with William I (the 'Conqueror', r. 1066–87) and ending with Stephen, (r. 1135–54). The first requirement of any student of this period is to obtain clear knowledge and an understanding of the familial relations of William the Conqueror. It is a complex tangle of relationships. The following exercise is designed to help you get your bearings. But first of all, it is important to know how to 'read' a family tree.

How to 'read' a family tree.

a) Vertical lines. Follow the line down to find the children of a marriage; follow the line up to find the parents and grandparents and so on of a particular individual.

b) Horizontal lines. The names shown on these lines (indicated by a very small vertical line (I)) are brothers and sisters. The firstborn appears on the far left of a horizontal line; the youngest is shown on the right.

c) '=' sign shows a marriage. Sometimes an individual has several marriages. If so, this is shown as (1), (2) and so on.

d) Where a name is shown in uppercase this means that the named individual governed as king or queen; the dates below the name show the period that this individual ruled

Questions

1) Study Source A

   a) Who was the wife of William the Conqueror?

   b) How many children were produced from the marriage of William the Conqueror?

   c) Who was the eldest of these children?

   d) Who was the youngest?

   e) Who was the maternal grandfather (i.e. mother's father) of Stephen of Blois?

2) From 1066, William I was king of England and duke of Normandy. William decided who would succeed him in each of these positions. Study carefully the family tree to work out who became king, and who became duke, immediately following William's death in 1087.

3) Why do you think William did not leave both positions to the same person?

4) One of the key criteria for claiming the throne was the possession of a blood relationship to previous kings through the male bloodline. Using this criterion, work in pairs and answer these questions:

   i) Upon the death of William I, which of either Robert Duke of Normandy or William Rufus had the stronger claim on the inheritance? Explain your answer.

   ii) Upon the death of Henry I, what claims to the throne might the Empress Matilda and Stephen of Blois have had? Explain your answer.

5) Consider your answers to each of questions 1–4. List the various factors which influenced who inherited the throne and leading dukedoms.

Source A. The Norman family tree, 1066–1154.

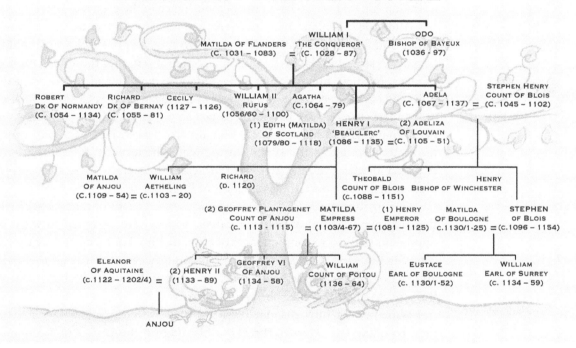

NORMAN FAMILY TREE

2) Who was William the Conqueror?

The exact date of William (the Conqueror's) birth is not known, though it occurred either in 1027 or 1028. His epithet, or nickname, 'the Bastard', refers to the fact that his parents were not married. He was the illegitimate child of a liaison (union) between his father, Duke Robert II of Normandy, and Herleva, the daughter of a tanner of Falaise in Normandy. Robert made William his heir because he had no living legitimate children when he died in 1035.

An heir who succeeded when still a child was unable to rule personally and so relied instead on a group of nominated adults to rule as a council until the heir was deemed to be old enough. This arrangement frequently created political instability and increased lawlessness, sometimes even leading to civil war. On several occasions William was forced to flee at short notice to avoid capture or worse by powerful lords seeking to seize his title. William Giroie, a lord from southern Normandy, attended a wedding feast given by another lord, William de Bellême, where he was attacked and badly disfigured: his eyes, ears and genitals were cut off. The only person capable of punishing de Bellême would have been an adult and a strong duke of Normandy.

William began to rule Normandy personally in his late teens and was able to impose some order on his duchy after his decisive victory over rebels at the battle of Val-es-Dunes in 1047. In the aftermath of the battle William proclaimed the Truce of God, which prohibited warfare at certain times and was supported by many other European rulers. This marked the beginning of a close association with the church, strengthened when William followed the custom of appointing men of his own choice as bishops, notably his half-brother Odo as bishop of Bayeux about 1050. William's personal support for the church in Normandy ensured good relations with the head of the church, the pope, resident in Rome, a relationship that was to have crucial importance in the events of 1066.

After 1047, William had effectively secured his control over Normandy, but he still faced several external threats from other powerful French nobles hoping to seize the duchy by military conquest. He met these in a number of ways. In 1050, his marriage to Matilda, the daughter of one of the most powerful of the great territorial princes of northern France, Count Baldwin V of Flanders (present-day Belgium), forged an influential alliance which would deter challenges to his authority. William also waged incessant war against his rivals throughout the 1050s, during which he learned the military skills required for effective campaigns and successful siegecraft. These skills were to play an important part in his conquest of England.

During these years William also demonstrated deeds of calculated cruelty that became a feature of his later career, which were designed to warn his opponents of the dire consequences of crossing him. For instance, having successfully besieged Alençon in 1052, William proceeded to cut off the hands and feet of those defenders who had hung furs and pelts (animal skins) from the walls to taunt the duke about his bastardy.

William was fully occupied until c.1060 with removing the internal, then reducing the external, threats to his hold on the Duchy of Normandy. Thereafter, he could contemplate challenging other lords and kings for their territories.

Question

1) Study Sources A and B. Use these sources and your own knowledge to explain how William imposed his authority on Normandy. You should mention the following in your answer:

- Battle of Val-es-Dunes
- Truce of God
- Matilda
- Character of William

Source A. Map showing Normandy.

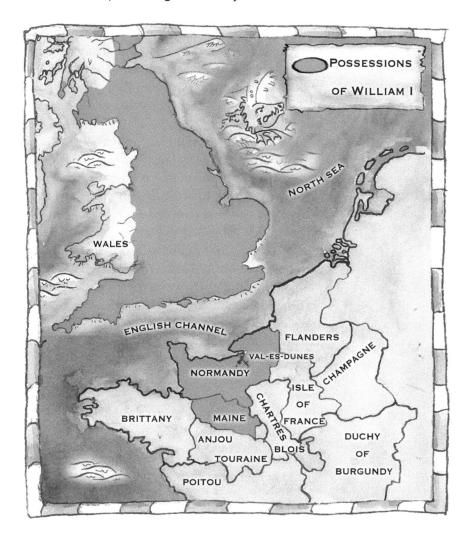

Source B. The Norman William of Poitiers (1020–c.1090) wrote his *Deeds of William, Duke of Normandy and King of England* about 1075–77. In his youth he was a soldier and later became a priest, eventually becoming William's personal chaplain.

> [At Val-es-Dunes] the greater part of the barons of Normandy followed the banner of disloyalty. But William was not alarmed by so many swords. Rushing in, he spread such terror by slaughter that his adversaries [enemies] lost heart and their arms weakened. The one thought that remained to them was to run away. William pursued them for some miles, punishing them relentlessly. This one-day battle was momentous, deserving to be remembered in future ages, for it set a terrible example, broke with iron the heads of the overbearing [barons] and the battlements of the wicked, threw down many castles with the impelling hand of victory, and put down civil war in our region for a long time.

3) Who was Matilda, wife of the Conqueror?

In 1050, William married Matilda, daughter of Baldwin V, count of Flanders. The marriage produced perhaps as many as nine children (records do not exist to establish the exact number definitively). Very unusually for the time, William does not seem to have taken any mistresses or produced any illegitimate children, which suggests that this arranged marriage was also a close and affectionate one.

William trusted Matilda. From 1066 she assumed significant political responsibility, acting as regent (a person who exercise ruling power in a kingdom when the monarch is absent or incapacitated) for her husband in Normandy during his frequent absences in England and exercising power in his stead. She was crowned queen of England in 1068 and was frequently present at William's thrice-annual crown-wearing ceremonies. Matilda was also the central figure within their family and was on excellent terms with her children. William's relations with his eldest son, Robert Curthose, were poor, and Matilda worked behind the scenes to improve them, such as sending significant quantities of silver and gold to Robert without William's knowledge. Robert's rebellion against William in 1078–80 caused her significant distress (see p. 166). All in all, the evidence demonstrates that Matilda played a central political and familial role typical of the most active medieval queens.

Question

1) Study Source A. What does this source reveal about Matilda's role as regent and her relationship with William?

Source A. A letter from William to Matilda.

> William, by the grace of God king of the English, to queen Matilda, his dear spouse, perpetual health/greeting. I want you to know that I grant to St. Martin at Marmontier the church of Ste. Marie des Pieux and the lands that depend on it, free of all rents, as priest Hugh held them on the day of his death. Furthermore, I charge you to render, as is just, all the land in Normandy belonging to St. Martin, free and secure from all those who would wish to burden it, as well as from the demands of the foresters; above all forbid Hugolin de Cherbourg to meddle further with the affairs of this house.

4) Who was Edward the Confessor?

Although King Alfred and his successors had enjoyed success against the Vikings, the Vikings had not given up their designs upon England. Ethelred (r. 978–1016) and his successor Edmund Ironside (r. 1016) were unable to resist assaults led by the Danish king Svein Forkbeard (king of England 1013–14) and his son, Cnut (r. 1016–35). The most legitimate contender for the throne in opposition to Cnut at this time was Edward (who later became known as the 'Confessor', because of his saintly reputation), Emma of Normandy's son from her marriage to Ethelred. (Refer to Source A on p. 84 and make sure that you can locate each of these rulers.) In 1016, when Cnut came to the throne, Edward was about 12 years old, and he fled to Normandy, where he remained for the next 20 years.

Cnut married Emma of Normandy, the widow of King Ethelred, which was a clever political move. You can see from the family tree (see Source A, p. 84) that it symbolically brought together Cnut's dynasty (family) with that of the rulers of Wessex, and strengthened his links with the Normans.

Crucially, as soon as the marriage of Cnut and Emma produced a son, Harthacnut (b. 1018), the claims of Ethelred's heirs to the throne were undermined because there were now two lines of legitimate offspring, all of whom were children of one of two kings of England and the same queen. Edward represented the Wessex line of kings, and he appeared to have lost this dynasty's hold on the Crown of England as he languished in exile at the court of his uncle, Duke Richard II of Normandy.

Questions

1) Study Source A. 'There could have been few better connected women of the time than Emma of Normandy'. In what ways does Source A support this statement?

2) Study Source A. Which one of the following do you think had the strongest claim to the throne in 1035: Edward the Atheling; Edward the Confessor; Harold Harefoot; Harthacnut; William. Explain your answer.

BRITISH DEPTH STUDIES C.500–1100

Source A. Family tree showing the Anglo-Saxon, Norman and Scandinavian lines of descent about the year 1000.

ROLLO

RICHARD II
DUKE OF NORMANDY 996 - 1026

ROBERT I
DUKE OF NORMANDY 1027 - 1035

(ILLEGITIMATE)

WILLIAM
THE CONQUEROR

} NORMAN

ALFRED THE GREAT

AELFGIFU = ETHELRED THE UNREADY = EMMA OF NORMANDY
R. 978 - 1013 AND 1014 - 1016
B. 989 R. 1016

EDMUND IRONSIDES

EDWARD THE CONFESSOR = EDITH
B. 1003

ALFRED
D. 1036

EDGAR THE ATHELING
D. 1120

EDWARD THE ATHELING
D. 1057

} ANGLO-SAXON

SVEIN

CNUT
R. 1016 - 1035

HAROLD
HAREFOOT
B. 1005C.
R.1035 - 1040

HARTHACNUT
B. 1018C
R. 1040 - 1042

} SCANDINAVIAN
(I.E. DENMARK AND NORWAY)

KEY:
B = BORN
D = DIED
R = REIGN

5) Why might Edward the Confessor have promised William the throne?

Edward was to remain in exile in Normandy for the best part of a quarter of a century, from c.1016 to 1035. His long residence in Normandy created an emerging sense that the Norman dukes were Edward's loyal supporters. This was reinforced in 1036 when Edward and his younger brother Alfred crossed the Channel and landed in England, having been encouraged by their mother to try and seize the throne after the death of Cnut late in 1035. However, Alfred fell into the hands of Godwin, a fierce Anglo-Saxon warrior figure whom Cnut had made Earl of Wessex in 1018. Under Godwin's orders, Arthur was blinded, and died as a result. Meanwhile, Edward appears to have enjoyed a successful hit-and-run raid, before returning out of Godwin's reach to Normandy. At this moment it must have seemed that in all probability a Scandinavian dynasty – descendants of Cnut – would cement itself as the ruling house of England.

In fact the successive and early deaths of Cnut's sons, Harold Harefoot (d.1040) and Harthacnut (d.1042), suddenly revived Edward's prospects. Edward had by chance become the most obvious contender for the throne, and he was duly crowned in Winchester on 3 April 1043. The old English line of Wessex had been restored.

Some historians argue that by the end of 1051 the childless Edward had nominated Duke William as his successor, most probably out of thanks for the many years of safety he spent in the household of the Dukes of Normandy. If this is true, William now had two claims to the throne: the nomination from the incumbent king, and his blood relationship with Edward through his great aunt, Emma of Normandy (Edward's mother).

Questions

1) Study Source A. Use this source and your own knowledge to explain why Edward may have nominated William as his successor in 1051.

2) Study Source A. How reliable do you consider this source? Explain your answer.

Source A. The Norman William of Poitiers (1020–c.1090) wrote his *Deeds of William, Duke of Normandy and King of England* about 1075–77. In his youth he was a soldier and later became a priest. He was not involved in the invasion of 1066. Here he describes what happened to Alfred when he was captured by Godwin in 1035.

> [Earl Godwin] rejoiced when he saw Alfred in chains and ordered the best of his companions to be beheaded in his presence. Godwin then put Alfred in shameful nakedness on a horse and had him led to the marshes so he could be tortured and starved. Godwin delighted in making the life of his enemy, Alfred, more burdensome than death. At the same time he intended to frighten Edward utterly with the sufferings of his brother. Thus perished this most beautiful youth for he could not survive long because while they were putting out his eyes with a knife the point damaged his brain.

6) Who were the Godwins?

Cnut had divided England into four great earldoms: Wessex, Mercia, East Anglia and Northumbria, over which he appointed earls to act as his agents. The most significant of these new appointments proved to be that of Godwin, an Anglo-Saxon raised to Earl of Wessex in 1018. The Godwins rose to become the most important family in the kingdom. and in 1066 Godwin's son, Harold, seized the throne.

Relations between Earl Godwin and King Edward were strained, because of Godwin's role in the murder of Alfred. Yet Edward depended upon Godwin's influence, authority and military power to help him rule England, especially while the threat of further invasions from various Scandinavian princes remained strong. Thus the Godwins benefitted enormously from royal patronage, so that almost all the offspring of Earl Godwin (at least eight in number, including Harold, Tostig and Swein) came to hold important positions at the royal court and large tracts of landed estates (See Source C on p. 90). Furthermore, in 1045 Edward married Godwin's daughter Edith, probably as part of the political price Edward had to pay for the Godwins' support.

Meanwhile, the focus of power within the Godwin clan shifted decisively in the late 1040s. In 1046, the eldest son, Swein, was disgraced for abducting the abbess of Leominster, and then in 1049 he was declared an outlaw for the shocking crime of murdering his cousin. At this point Harold, the second eldest, became his father's most important lieutenant.

Question

1) Study Source A. Use the contents of Source A and your own knowledge to explain the presence of Tostig and Harold in this picture even though Edward the Confessor had reason to detest the Godwins.

Source A. An illustration from the mid-thirteenth-century *Life of Edward the Confessor* showing brothers Tostig and Harold (the future King Harold II) fighting, bottom right, at a feast hosted by King Edward the Confessor.

i) The year 1051 – the Godwins in trouble

In these circumstances it was inevitable that at some point the childless Edward would seek to diminish the influence of the Godwins by strengthening his own spheres of influence, and that to do so he should turn to the connections he had made during his exile in Normandy. He therefore promoted Normans to positions in the English church, notably Robert of Jumièges, who was made archbishop of Canterbury in 1051.

The appointment of Robert of Jumieges led to a showdown with the Godwins, who now felt their influence to be threatened. This showdown was triggered by uncontrolled lawlessness at Dover in September 1051, when the townsfolk fought with the supporters of Eustace of Boulogne, the king's brother-in-law, who was returning to France after a visit to Edward. The king called upon Earl Godwin, who as Earl of Wessex was responsible for Dover, to punish its inhabitants. Godwin refused, because he was outraged at the appointment of Robert of Jumièges and was quietly supportive of the violent actions of the Dover men. Edward responded by preparing for war against the rebellious Earl of Wessex, drawing upon the support of Siward and Leofric,

Earls of Northumbria and Mercia respectively. The king's action was enough to force the Godwins to flee the country, and he consolidated his victory by renouncing his wife Edith, Godwin's daughter. It seemed as though the Godwins had been broken and defeated.

ii) The Godwins' fortunes improve

Edward's quarrel had been with Earl Godwin himself, and so the earl's death in 1053 proved a watershed, enabling the rest of the family to regroup and re-establish themselves. Harold succeeded his father to the earldom of Wessex and during the 1050s significantly consolidated his authority – indeed, one source refers to him at this time as *subregulus*, 'under-king'. The territorial holdings of the family were also substantially increased, especially when in 1055 Harold's brother Tostig was elevated to the great earldom of Northumberland after the death of Siward. About this time their brothers Gyrth and Leofwine were given the earldoms of East Anglia and Kent respectively.

In total, the Godwins controlled over twice the amount of land held by the family of Earl Leofric of Mercia, the next wealthiest family in England, and 20 times as much as the kingdom's wealthiest thegnly families. No king could rule without their support, but, equally, the great and growing ambition of the Godwins meant that it was increasingly difficult to rule with them.

Meanwhile, Edward the Atheling, the son of Edmund Ironside (d.1016), returned to England from Hungary in 1057 only to die upon his arrival. This Edward had by far the strongest hereditary (i.e. blood) claim upon the throne, given that the king remained childless. His son, Edgar the Atheling, was only a few years old. At this point, Harold may have begun to aim for the crown.

Questions

1) Study Sources A and B. How far do these sources agree on i) the reasons for the exile of the Godwins and ii) the reasons for their return?

2) How can you explain the degree of disagreement between these sources? Explain your answer.

3) Identify and explain the extent to which the fortunes of the Godwins fluctuated during the reign of Edward the Confessor?

4) Study Sources C, D and E. Use Sources C, D and E and your own know-ledge to describe the extent to which the Godwin family represented a threat to Edward the Confessor by 1066.

Source A. From the *Life of King Edward*. Probably composed between 1065 and 1067 by a monk in the household of Queen Edith.

> The archbishop [i.e. Robert of Jumieges], having attained a dignity of the highest honour, began to irritate and oppose the earl [of Wessex i.e. Godwin] with all his power. There were frequent controversies between them because Robert said that Godwin had invaded his lands and had damaged them by holding them for his own use. However, the industrious earl bore the heedless fury of the bishop peacefully but, adding madness to madness, with all his effort Robert turned the king's mind against Godwin [by alleging that Godwin had been responsible for the death of the king's brother, Alfred, in 1035 and so] the earl was driven into exile. All the English honoured Godwin as a father [and so when they heard that he had gone into exile they were] terrified by the news of his sudden departure. They believed his absence to herald their own ruin, the destruction of the English people, indeed, the downfall of the whole land. [Eventually Godwin returned] and all came to meet him, like children their long-awaited father.

Source B. Eadmer's *History of Recent Events in England*. Eadmer (d. c.1126) was an English monk at Christ Church, Canterbury.

> At that time Godwin, Earl of Wessex, was throughout all England accounted a great man on land and sea. But a serious quarrel arose between him and the king and he was condemned to exile with all his family [in Flanders]. After the death of Emma, the king's mother, Godwin and Harold returned to England, each escorted by a large number of ships and a strong force of soldiers. [Many nobles wanted to make peace] but the king, suspicious of Godwin, would not consent to peace unless he were first given hostages as security. [Members of the Godwin family were given as hostages and were] despatched to Normandy to the guardianship of Duke William. After these events Godwin, a bitter enemy of the Church of Canterbury (for he was guilty of stealing her lands) shortly afterwards died an evil death.

Source C. A graphical representation of the value of lands held by the king and leading families in 1066.

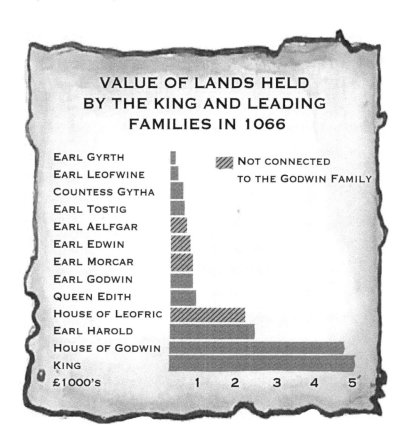

Source D. A map showing the location and scale of the earldoms in 1065.

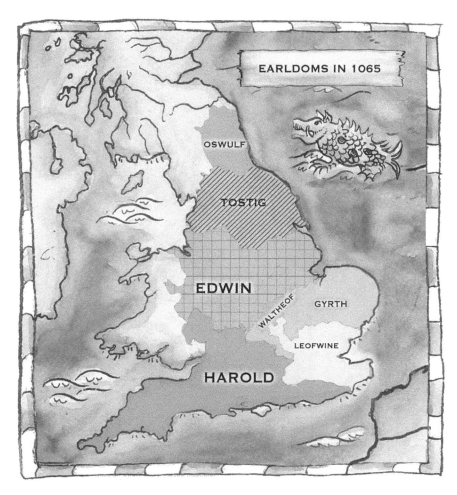

Source E. A map showing the distribution of the land holding of Harold in 1066.

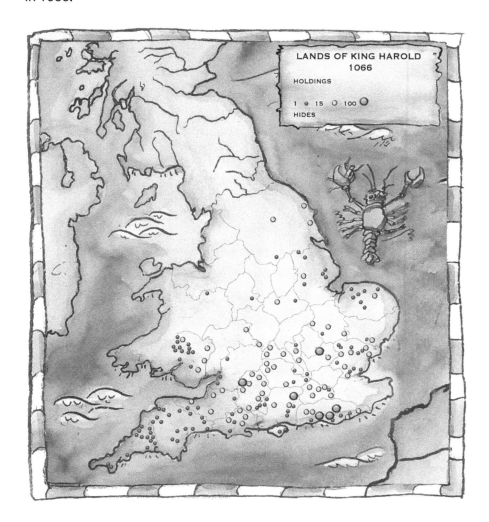

---

7) How did William's situation improve in 1064?

Several developments now occurred which meant that William would be in a position to press his claim to the English throne. The most significant was a series of events which reduced the external threats to William's control over the Duchy of Normandy, which meant that he was no longer permanently occupied with political events in France. The deaths of his leading rivals in the early 1060s was followed in 1064 by William's successful invasion of the neighbouring county of Maine, which secured the southern border of Normandy. Furthermore, in 1064 William was presented with the person of Harold Godwinson by Guy, Count of Ponthieu, who had captured Harold while the latter was travelling in northern France.

Norman sources written after the event claim that Harold had been sent to William (by Edward) to confirm Edward's promise of the succession to William. There is no confirmation of this in any contemporary English source, and it seems more likely that Harold went to France for other reasons. Whatever the cause of his visit, Norman sources allege that whilst in Normandy Harold took an oath of fealty (loyalty) to William, promising upon holy relics to respect the latter's claim to the English throne – a scene vividly depicted in the Bayeux tapestry. (See Source D, p. 95) Therefore, from the Norman perspective, when Harold took the throne upon the death of Edward in January 1066, he did so as a usurper (someone who seizes power) and a perjurer (oath breaker).

Source Investigation. Harold's embassy to William, 1064. Study Sources A–E and answer these questions:

1) Study Sources A and B. What reasons do these sources give for i) Edward sending Harold to Normandy in 1064 and ii) why he chose Harold for this embassy?

2) Study Source C. What can you learn from this source about the details of the oath taken by Harold?

3) Study Sources C and D. What can you learn from Source D about the 'sacred ritual' referred to in Source C?

3) Study Sources C and E. i) To what extent do these sources agree as to whether Harold took the oath of his own free will? ii) How can you account for any disagreement? Explain your answer.

4) Study Source F. How convincing do you consider Douglas's interpretation of Harold's action? Use your contextual knowledge to explain your answer.

> **Source A. The *Deeds of the Norman Dukes* by William of Jumieges (d. c.1070), written c.1070. William was a monk in the abbey at Jumieges in Normandy.**
>
> Edward, king of the English, being, according to the will of God, without an heir, sent Robert [of Jumièges], archbishop of Canterbury to the duke of Normandy, with a message appointing the duke as heir to the kingdom which God had entrusted to him. He also at a later time sent to the duke, Harold, the greatest of all the men in his kingdom alike in riches and honour and power. This he did in order that Harold might guarantee the crown to the duke by his fealty and confirm the same with an oath according to Christian usage. [Having fallen into the hands of Guy, Count of Ponthieu, duke William forced Harold to be released.] Harold thereupon spent some time with William, and performed fealty to him in respect of the kingdom [of England] with many oaths. After this the duke sent him back to the king with many gifts.
>
> **Source B. The Norman William of Poitiers (1020–c.1090) wrote his *Deeds of William, Duke of Normandy and King of England* about 1075–77. In his**

youth he was a soldier and later became a priest. **He was not involved in the invasion of 1066.**

[Around the time 1063–64] Edward, king of the English, who loved William, Duke of Normandy as a brother or a son, established him as heir with a stronger pledge than ever before. He therefore sent Harold to William in order that he might confirm his promise by oath. This Harold was of all the king's subjects the richest and most exalted in honour and power, and his brother and his cousins had previously been offered as hostages in respect of the same succession. The king, indeed, here acted with great prudence [wiseness] in choosing Harold for this task, in the hope that the riches and the authority of this most important man might check disturbance throughout England if the people with their accustomed perfidy [lack of trust] should be disposed to overturn what had been determined.

Source C. The Norman William of Poitiers (1020–c.1090) wrote his *Deeds of William, Duke of Normandy and King of England* about 1075–77. In his youth he was a soldier and later became a priest. He was not involved in the invasion of 1066.

[Harold, having been shipwrecked on the coast of Ponthieu and captured by Count Guy], William secured his honourable release and then took Harold with proper honour to Rouen. When they arrived at Bonneville, Harold in that place swore fealty to the duke employing the sacred ritual recognised amongst Christian men. And as is testified by the most truthful and honourable men who were there present, he took an oath of his own free will in the following terms: firstly that he would be the representative of Duke William at the court of his lord, King Edward, as long as the king lived; secondly that he would employ all his influence and wealth to ensure that after the death of King Edward the kingdom of England should be confirmed in the possession of the duke; thirdly that he would place a garrison of the duke's knights in the castle of Dover; fourthly that in other parts of England at the pleasure of the duke he would maintain garrisons in other castles and make complete provision for their well-being.

Source D. An artist's impression of a scene from the Bayeux Tapestry showing Harold performing fealty. The Tapestry was commissioned by Bishop Odo, the half-brother of William. It seems to have been produced in England in the early 1070s.

Source E. Eadmer's *History of Recent Events in England*. Eadmer (d. c.1126) was an English monk at Christ Church Canterbury.

[When Harold was in Normandy, William told him] that Edward, years before when Edward was detained with him in Normandy, when they were both young, that Edward had promised him he would make over to William the right to succeed him on the throne as his heir. [William thus said that Harold, upon the death of Edward, must do all that he could to allow William to become king.] Harold realised that here was danger whatever way he turned. He could not see any way of escape without agreeing to all that William wished. So he agreed. Then William, to ensure that everything should be firmly ratified, had relics of saints brought out and made Harold swear over them that he would indeed implement all which they had agreed. [When Harold returned and told Edward] the king exclaimed: 'Did I not tell you that I knew William and that your going might bring untold calamity upon this kingdom?'

Source F. From *William the Conqueror* by D. C. Douglas. p. 177.

It is not impossible that Harold willingly consented to what took place [in Normandy], and perhaps even he acted here on his own initiative. The perils which surrounded his own designs [i.e. plans] on the English throne were very obvious, for such an attempt could only succeed if he could obtain sufficient support at home to override the rights of surviving members of the English royal house and the claims of strong Scandinavian princes. Harold may thus perhaps have thought to safeguard his future position in the event of his own failure or the duke's success. And he may have felt that in any case he could later repudiate the oath, or plead that it had been taken under compulsion.

8) Why did Tostig go into exile in 1065?

Tostig, Harold's brother, had been made Earl of Northumbria in 1055, and thereafter had acted as a trusted minister of Edward and had provided loyal service to the crown. He had also assisted Harold. For instance, in 1063 he supported Harold's assault upon Wales. The success of the campaign probably encouraged the Welsh to kill their king, Gruffudd ap Llywelyn, and present his head to Harold and Tostig to appease them.

Although Tostig maintained good relations with both king and brother, his rule in Northumbria became fierce and oppressive. He introduced high taxes and probably sought to introduce West Saxon law into a region that had become accustomed to governing itself. When two thegns, Gamel and Ulf, met with Tostig to complain about these impositions, the earl had them arrested and executed. In the same year Tostig ordered the murder of another important nobleman called Gospatric. These actions prompted a rebellion. On 3 October 1065, a group of rebels broke into Tostig's residence in York and nominated Morcar as Earl of Northumbria, whose brother Edwin was already Earl of Mercia. The rebels then marched south. They met with representatives of Edward, demanding that Edward recognize Morcar in place of Tostig. However, Edward ignored their demands and ordered that Harold, Tostig's brother, march north and put down the rebellion. Harold's response displayed great political cunning. He refused the king's order because he did not wish to begin a civil war and he realized that he would benefit not only from winning the support of Morcar and Edwin but also from his brother's demise as earl. Tostig thus went into exile, travelling first to Flanders and then Denmark and Norway. He was determined upon revenge and in 1066 launched a series of attacks on England, eventually allying with Harald Hardrada, King of Norway, with whom he was defeated and killed by Harold at the Battle of Stamford Bridge on 25 September. (See p. 108.)

Questions

1) Study Source A. What does this source suggest about the authority of Edward the Confessor, and how surprising do you find this? Explain your answer.

2) Study Source B. Use the details of this source and your own knowledge to explain why Harold had a motive to support the interests of Morcar.

Source A. Florence of Worcester was an early twelfth century chronicler. Here he describes the refusal of leading men to restore Tostig as Earl of Northumbria.

> 1065: [After taking York] nearly all the men in the earldom [of Northumbria] assembled and went to Northampton to meet Harold, earl of Wessex, and others whom the king, at Tostig's request, had sent to restore peace amongst them. There, as also afterwards at Oxford they unanimously refused and they outlawed Tostig and all who had taken part with him in his unjust government. After the Feast of All Saints [1 November], with the agreement of Earl Edwin, they banished Tostig from England.

Source B. Family tree showing the Godwins' relationship to other important families.

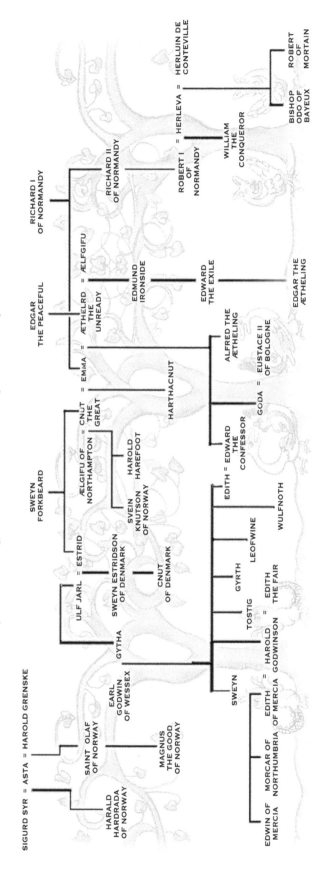

9) What was the impact of the death of Edward the Confessor?

Edward the Confessor died on 5 January 1066. English writers at the time claimed that with his last breath he nominated Harold to be his successor. If so, this clarified any uncertainly about the succession, and it certainly overrode any claim by William that he had been nominated in 1051. Harold closed down any possible debate by his rapid coronation the very next day, either by Archbishop Ealdred of York or by Stigand, archbishop of Canterbury. (Stigand had usurped – taken without agreement – the office of archbishop and had therefore fallen out with the pope.) Harold was crowned, and Edward was buried, in Westminster Abbey on the same day.

The unusual haste of proceedings reflected the prevailing air of unease and indicates that Harold fully expected a challenge to his acquisition of the throne. An earl with no legitimate claim to royal descent had grabbed power. The sense of foreboding was enhanced by the appearance of a comet. The *Anglo-Saxon Chronicle* recorded that at this time 'all over England there was seen a sign in the skies such as had never been seen before'.

Harold's actions amounted to a coup d'état (a seizing of power) to which any other claimant to the throne, such as Duke William, was bound to respond.

Questions

1) Study Source A. What can you learn from this source about the rules and realities of succession to the Crown in 1066?

2) Study Source B.

   i) Why do you think the Bayeux Tapestry shows Stigand(t) as the archbishop presiding over the ceremony when other sources suggest that this role was performed by Ealdred? Use your own knowledge and the source to explain your answer.

   ii) In light of your answer to i), what does this tell you about the propaganda, purpose and power of the Bayeux Tapestry?

3) Study Source C. Use the details of Source C and your own knowledge to write a report for William of Normandy, advising him of the leading figures in England at the time of the death of Edward the Confessor.

Source A. The *Life of St Edward the Confessor* by St Aelred of Rievaulx, an English monk. Written in the 1160s.

[Upon the death of Edward] the island was filled with tears and woe. When he had been buried as befitted such a one as he – in Westminster abbey as I have mentioned – some attempted to elect as king Edgar the Atheling, to whom the kingdom was due by right of descent. But since the child was thought unsuitable for such an honour, in a tragic mistake earl Harold obtained the kingdom, but only because he was more astute mentally, his purse was deeper and his troops more numerous.

Source B. An artist's impression of a scene from the Bayeux Tapestry showing the crowning of Harold on 6 January 1066. The Tapestry was commissioned by Bishop Odo, the half-brother of William. It seems to have been produced in England in the early 1070s.

Source C. Map showing Northern Europe on the death of Edward the Confessor.

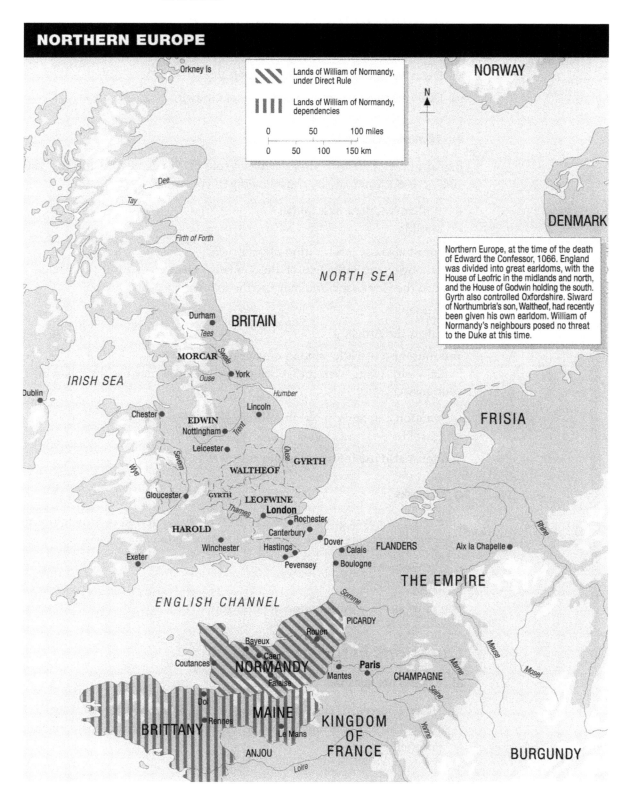

NORTHERN EUROPE

Lands of William of Normandy, under Direct Rule

Lands of William of Normandy, dependencies

0   50   100 miles
0   50   100   150 km

N

NORWAY

DENMARK

Orkney Is

Dee

Tay

Firth of Forth

NORTH SEA

Durham

BRITAIN

Tees

MORCAR

Swale

York

IRISH SEA

Ouse

Humber

Dublin

Chester

Lincoln

EDWIN

Nottingham

Trent

Leicester

Ouse

GYRTH

Severn

WALTHEOF

Wye

Gloucester

GYRTH

LEOFWINE

Thames

London

Rochester

HAROLD

Canterbury

Winchester

Hastings

Dover

Exeter

Pevensey

Calais

Boulogne

FLANDERS

FRISIA

Rhine

Aix la Chapelle

THE EMPIRE

ENGLISH CHANNEL

Somme

PICARDY

Rouen

Bayeux

Coutances

Caen

NORMANDY

Paris

Mantes

CHAMPAGNE

Marne

Meuse

Mosel

Falaise

Dol

MAINE

Rennes

BRITTANY

Le Mans

KINGDOM OF FRANCE

ANJOU

Loire

Yonne

BURGUNDY

Seine

Northern Europe, at the time of the death of Edward the Confessor, 1066. England was divided into great earldoms, with the House of Leofric in the midlands and north, and the House of Godwin holding the south. Gyrth also controlled Oxfordshire. Siward of Northumbria's son, Waltheof, had recently been given his own earldom. William of Normandy's neighbours posed no threat to the Duke at this time.

10) Exam practice and online resources

Questions in the style of Edexcel

a) 4 marks per question

i) Describe two features of an oath of fealty

ii) Describe two features of the House of Godwin

b) 12 marks per question

Explain how William consolidated his rule in Normandy during the years 1047–c.1060. You may use the following in your answer:

- William's actions as a soldier
- Matilda

You must also use information of your own.

Explain why the influence of the Godwins increased during the reign of Edward the Confessor. You may use the following in your answer:

- Edith
- Edgar the Atheling

You must also use information of your own.

Explain why Tostig went into rebellion in 1065. You may use the following in your answer:

- taxation demands in Northumbria
- Harold

You must also use information of your own.

c) 16 marks

'The reign of Edward the Confessor 1043–66 was a period of growing crisis'. How far do you agree? You may use the following in your answer:

- the Godwins
- Duke William

You must also use information of your own.

Questions in the style of AQA

a) 8 marks per question

i) Study Source A. How convincing is this interpretation of Harold in 1065? Explain your answer using Interpretation A and your contextual knowledge.

Source A. David Carpenter. *The Struggle for Mastery* (2003).

> [Harold] was a clever politician: in 1065 he condoned, if not encouraged, the northern rebellion against his brother Tostig, earl in Northumbria since 1055, and had thereby removed a rival, conciliated the north and made alliance with the only family whose wealth remotely approached his own, that of Edwin, earl in Mercia, and his brother Morcar, who succeeded Tostig as earl in the north.

ii) Study Source B. How convincing is this interpretation of the coronation of Harold in January 1066? Explain your answer using Interpretation B and your contextual knowledge.

Source B. A modern artist's impression of the coronation of Harold.

iii) Study Source C. How convincing is this interpretation of the preparations for the invasion of England ordered by William? Explain your answer using Interpretation C and your contextual knowledge.

Source C. A modern artist's impression of the preparations for invasion ordered by Duke William.

b) 8 marks per question

i) Explain why some historians believe that Edward the Confessor nominated William as his successor as early as 1051.

ii) Explain how the authority of the Godwins fluctuated between 1051 and 1052.

iii) Explain the significance of Edward the Confessor's death on 5 January 1066.

c) 8 marks per question

i) Write an account of Edward's experiences during the years 1016–43.

ii) Write an account showing how William's circumstances improved from 1060 to 1065.

iii) Write an account of Harold's experiences during his visit to Normandy in 1064.

Online Resources

Useful biography of the Earl Godwin http://www.englishmonarchs.co.uk/saxon_30.html.

Clear images of the entire Bayeux Tapestry http://hastings1066.com/baythumb.shtml.

4 THE YEAR 1066: WILLIAM WINS ENGLAND

Key Issues

Timeline

1066

5 January: Death of Edward the Confessor

6 January: Coronation of Harold

May–June: Tostig launches attacks on England.

20 September: Tostig and Harald Hardrada defeat Morcar and Edwin at Gate Fulford.

25 September: Harold defeats Harald Hardrada and Tostig at Stamford Bridge.

28 September: William lands at Pevensey.

6 October: Harold enters London.

14 October: Battle of Hastings.

25 December: William crowned at Westminster Abbey

Overview

'The Battle of Hastings, 1066' is the best known date in English history. This chapter provides an outline of the key events that led up to the battle on 14 October. It explains the claims upon the English throne made not only by William and Harold but also by Harald Hardrada, king of Norway. It also outlines the importance of the other key battles of 1066, especially that fought at Stamford Bridge on 25 September 1066. Finally, it provides evidence to explain why William won at Hastings and discusses the actions he took in the months immediately following events at the battle to stamp his authority upon England. Although William had succeeded in eliminating Harold, gaining complete control of the kingdom would be an even greater challenge. As dawn broke on 15 October it was by no means inevitable that Norman rule would be successfully implemented throughout England.

1) What did William do upon learning of the death of Edward the Confessor?

William's immediate reaction to the news of Harold's coronation is not known, though it can be readily imagined. The Bayeux Tapestry, however, shows William receiving the information calmly, no doubt while in the process of instructing that a formal protest be sent to the English court.

Over the course of the next few months William ensured that he gained the support of his leading men for the proposed invasion, by seeking their counsel and by promising spoils, especially in the form of English land; he appealed to public opinion both within and without Normandy; and he raised an army, ensured that it was provided with ships and supplies to travel to England and that it possessed the equipment to fight when it arrived.

Source Investigation. William prepares to invade. Study Sources A–C.

1) Study Source A.

   a) Draw your own version of Source A. Label each of the following on your diagram:

      • swords

      • lances

      • axes

      • helmets

      • Hauberks

      • wine cask

b) How are the hauberks being carried? What does this suggest about their construction?

2) Study Sources A and C. Which of Sources A or C do you consider most useful for a historian investigating William's preparations? Explain your answer.

3) Study Sources A–C. Use these sources and your own knowledge to describe the preparations made by William for his invasion of England.

Source A. An artist's impression of a scene from Bayeux Tapestry showing the Normans carrying weapons and supplies to their ships. Scholars cannot agree upon the provenance of the Tapestry. The Tapestry was commissioned by Bishop Odo, the half-brother of William. It seems to have been produced in England in the early 1070s.

Source B. William of Poitiers. The Norman William of Poitiers (1020–c.1090) wrote his *Deeds of William, Duke of Normandy and King of England* about 1075–77. In his youth he was a soldier and later became a priest. He was not involved in the invasion of 1066.

Having taken counsel [advice] with his men, [Duke William] resolved to avenge the insult [of Harold taking the crown] by force of arms and to regain his inheritance by war. It would be tedious to tell in detail how by his prudent [wise] acts ships were made, arms and troops, provisions and other equipment assembled for war, and how the enthusiasm of the whole of Normandy was directed towards this enterprise. Nor did he neglect to take measures for the administration and the security of the duchy [of Normandy] during his absence. Further, many warriors came to his support from outside the duchy, some being attracted by his well-known generosity, and all by confidence in the justice of his cause. [William] forbade pillage, and provided for 50,000 soldiers at his own cost for a whole month while contrary winds delayed them at the mouth of the River Dives. ... The duke sought the favour of the pope for the project he had in hand, and gladly received from him the gift of a banner as a pledge for the support of St Peter whereby he might the more confidently and safely attack his enemy. With Henry, the Holy Roman Emperor, he entered into a new friendship so that an edict [agreement] was issued by which Germany might come to his aid if he asked for it against any enemy.

Source C. *The Deeds of the Norman Dukes* **by William of Jumièges. This section was written about 1070. William was a monk in the abbey at Jumièges in Normandy.**

[William] hastily built a fleet of 3,000 ships. At length he brought this fleet to anchor at St Valery in Ponthieu where he filled it with mighty horses and most valiant men with hauberks and helmets.

2) Who was Harald Hardrada and what happened in the Battles of Gate Fulford and Stamford Bridge?

The first assaults that Harold experienced were not led by William but by the new king's exiled brother, Tostig, seeking to redeem his position as Earl of Northumbria after having been driven into exile by a popular rebellion and succeeded by Harold's ally Morcar. Thwarted in his attacks on the south and east coast in May and June, Tostig joined forces with Harald Hardrada, King of Norway (r. 1047–66). It was a formidable pairing. As king of Norway, Harald pursued the claim to the Danish throne that his predecessor had made since 1041. Although Harald never became king of Denmark, he claimed that, as the legitimate successor to the Danish kings, he also possessed a claim to the English throne. The dispute over the succession in England in 1066 gave him the opportunity to try to fulfil his claim through an expedition – the last really major Viking assault upon England.

Despite these developments Harold concentrated his forces on the south coast, anticipating that William would invade before Harald and Tostig, but contrary winds delayed William's attempts to cross the Channel. Meanwhile, Harald Hardrada and Tostig landed at Riccal in Yorkshire in early September. On 20 September they drove off Earl Morcar and his brother, Edwin, Earl of Mercia, at the Battle of Gate Fulford outside York.

Upon receiving the news of the invasion in the north, Harold set forth on an extraordinary forced march of some two hundred miles. On 25 September he comprehensively defeated the invaders at Stamford Bridge, Harald and Tostig dying on the field of battle – though victory was achieved without the help of either Edwin or Morcar. (Nor did they present themselves at Hastings.) Such was the scale of the slaughter that of the 300 ships that Harald had employed for the invasion, only 24 were required for the survivors to take flight. However, Harold had little time to enjoy his victory: even as the sound of battle was dying away, the king was brought the news that William had landed at Pevensey on the south coast.

Task

1) Make a copy of the map shown in Source A. Add to it the key details related in the two paragraphs above. (Some details are already shown.)

Source A. A map showing the movements of William, Harold, Tostig and Harald Hardrada in 1066.

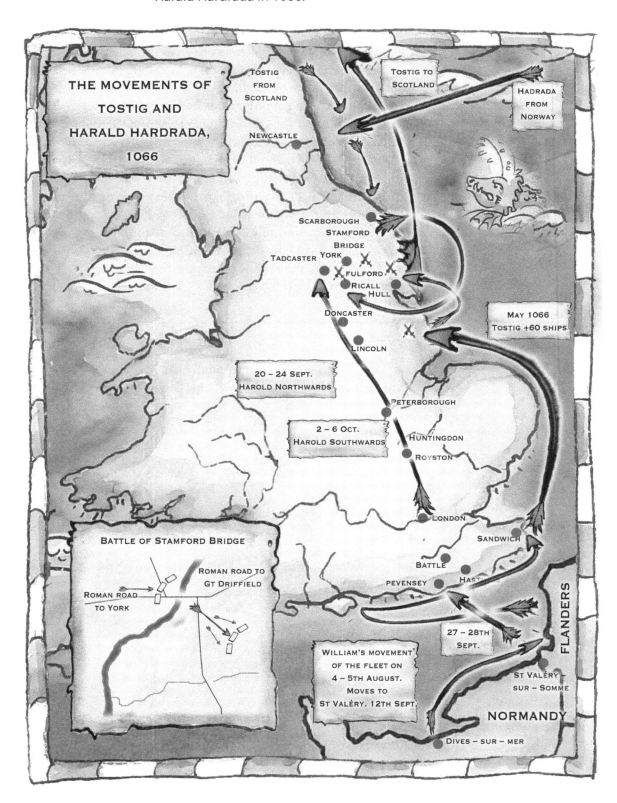

THE MOVEMENTS OF
TOSTIG AND
HARALD HARDRADA,
1066

TOSTIG FROM SCOTLAND

TOSTIG TO SCOTLAND

HADRADA FROM NORWAY

NEWCASTLE

SCARBOROUGH
STAMFORD BRIDGE
TADCASTER   YORK
FULFORD
RICALL
HULL
DONCASTER

LINCOLN

MAY 1066
TOSTIG +60 SHIPS

20 – 24 SEPT.
HAROLD NORTHWARDS

PETERBOROUGH

2 – 6 OCT.
HAROLD SOUTHWARDS

HUNTINGDON
ROYSTON

LONDON

SANDWICH

BATTLE OF STAMFORD BRIDGE

ROMAN ROAD TO
Gt DRIFFIELD

ROMAN ROAD
TO YORK

BATTLE

PEVENSEY   HAST...

FLANDERS

27 – 28TH
SEPT.

WILLIAM'S MOVEMENT
OF THE FLEET ON
4 – 5TH AUGUST.
MOVES TO
ST VALÉRY. 12TH SEPT.

ST VALÉRY –
SUR – SOMME

NORMANDY

DIVES – SUR – MER

3) How strong were the respective claims to the throne of the main claimants upon the death of Edward the Confessor?

By the mid-eleventh century two factors needed to be present to ensure a peaceful succession to the throne: a blood relationship to previous kings through the male bloodline, and acceptance by the English nobles. The latter was likely to be won by a claimant who could provide the type of strong leadership required of an English king, particularly in periods of military instability. Indeed, a renowned warrior backed by military might could make a powerful claim in the absence of other factors.

Questions

	1) Hereditary right /10	2) Designation by a reigning monarch /10	3) Military ability /10	Total /30
William				
Harold				
Edgar the Atheling (see p. 88)				
Harald Hardrada				

1) Copy and complete the table above, awarding a mark/10 against each of the three main criteria. Using the outcomes of this exercise, who do you think had the best claim upon the throne in 1066? Explain your answer.

2) Do you think that each of the criteria 1–3 shown in the table is of equal importance? Explain your answer.

3) Explain why there was a disputed succession when Edward the Confessor died. You may wish to refer to the following in your answer:

    i) uncertainty about the rules of succession

    ii) promises made by Edward

    iii) actions of Harold Godwin

    iv) actions of Hardrada

4) How secure was Harold as king in a) January 1066; b) after the Battle of Gate Fulford; c) after the Battle of Stamford Bridge? Explain your answer.

5) Study Source A. How far do you agree with this interpretation? Explain your answer.

Source A. David Carpenter. *The Struggle for Mastery* (2003).

[When Harold became king] his difficulties lay not with the state he inherited but with his political position. His alliance with Edwin and Morcar was fragile, despite his marriage to their sister. His brother Tostig in exile plotted revenge. Nothing could give Harold the prestige of the ancient House of Wessex [enjoyed by predecessors such as Alfred the Great.]

4) What happened at the Battle of Hastings, 14 October 1066?

Three days after Harold's success at Stamford Bridge on 25 September, the wind at last changed in William's favour and the duke landed on 28 September at Pevensey on the south coast where he quickly erected a fort within the old Roman fortification on that site. William's strategy now was not to stray far from the coast, thereby ensuring that he kept in touch with his ships. He also ravaged the surrounding countryside, partly as a means to provision his troops but also to advertise Harold's apparent inability to protect the people of Wessex – a form of psychological warfare that perhaps did much to lure Harold into battle on William's terms.

Meanwhile, Harold had entered London on 6 October with a force diminished by the impact of battle and the energy-sapping 200-mile march from Stamford Bridge. Nevertheless, so long as he was secure behind the still-intact Roman walls of London, there was much to be said for the king remaining in the city to regroup and to attract the enemy to him, and in doing so stretching William's supply lines and cutting off the invaders from their ships. Instead, emboldened by his victory in the north, and resentful of the damage being inflicted upon his earldom, Harold set out from London on 11 October.

The Norman and English forces engaged each other on 14 October some 11 kilometres northwest of Hastings, near the present-day town of Battle – a settlement that grew up around Battle Abbey, founded by William on the site of the battle. (Despite this, the battle that took place on 14 October is generally referred to as the Battle of Hastings.) Not yet replenished in number since the northern battles, and fatigued by the 60-mile march from London, the English took up position on the top of Senlac Hill. Here they established a shield wall so tightly knit that once battle commenced, the dead could not fall to the ground.

William appears to have arranged his forces in three groups: the Bretons on the left; the Normans in the centre and the French on the right. The front line was made up of archers with infantry directly behind. The knights were held in reserve. The papal banner hung above the heads of the Normans, an important propaganda device demonstrating that William led an invasion that had the support of the pope. At some point William placed around his neck the holy relics upon which Harold had sworn in 1064 when in Normandy.

Task

1) Using the previous four paragraphs, created a detailed timeline showing the key developments between 25 September and 14 October 1066.

2) Use the two paragraphs above to sketch an outline of the topography (i.e. the shape and features of the land) of the battlefield and the disposition of the forces of each side.

As with most medieval battles, it is hard for historians to know numbers involved in the Battle of Hastings, though most accept that neither side had more than 7,000 men. The English forces were composed entirely of infantry, the huscarls (superior infantry who fought with a large axe, sometimes double-headed) and the fyrd. The Normans had squadrons of mounted knights equipped with hauberks and helmets, and with swords or javelins. The Norman infantry was equipped with swords, javelins or long spears. William also had far more archers and crossbowmen than his enemy.

The battle lasted from dawn until dusk, suggesting that Hastings was a hard-fought battle between two armies essentially equal in strength. The English shield wall for much of the engagement proved impenetrable to the Normans, even to the knights. Eventually, a general Norman retreat initiated by the Bretons seems to have occurred when a rumour developed that William had been killed. This in turn encouraged the English to break from the shield wall in order to pursue those in flight, though this ended in an English rout and William raising his helmet to show that he was still alive. Perhaps inspired by this sequence of events, William seems to have adopted the tactic of feigned flight – in other words, purposefully fleeing in order to draw the English down the hill and to break the integrity of Harold's shield wall before halting and fighting. This in turn meant that the Norman archers became much more effective, no longer having to shoot uphill. It was probably at this point in the battle that Harold was killed, perhaps by an arrow in the eye as the Bayeux Tapestry seems to show, though the scene allows for more than one interpretation and it is confirmed by no reliable written source.

The death of the king signalled the end of the battle. The engagement had been attritional and bloody – Harold's body was so mutilated that it was identified only by his mistress, Edith Swan-neck, who alone knew of its secret marks. As we have seen William later ordered the building of an abbey on the site of the engagement – and called it Battle Abbey – with the altar located where Harold's body was found. Harold's brothers Gyrth and Leofwine also died in the battle. As dusk fell on the evening of 14 October Anglo-Saxon England was without a leader.

Questions

1)

    a) Study Sources A i)–iv). These are all scenes from the Bayeux Tapestry. Work in pairs and make certain that you can identify each of the following in the Tapestry:

- huscarls
- javelins/spears
- Senlac Hill
- hauberks
- archers
- arrows
- knights
- fyrd
- Harold – death
- sword
- axes
- stripping of the dead
- William raising his helmet

    b) Use your own knowledge to identify any confusion and/or errors in these scenes.

    c) Do these scenes appear to be in the correct sequence? Explain your answer.

2) Study Source B. How convincing is this interpretation of the Battle of Hastings? Explain your answer using Interpretation A and your contextual knowledge.

Source A i)–iv). A modern artist's impression of the Bayeux Tapestry. The Tapestry was commissioned by Bishop Odo, the half-brother of William. It seems to have been produced in England in the early 1070s.

Source A i)

Source A ii)

Source A iii)

Source A iv)

Source B. A modern artist's impression of the Battle of Hastings.

5) Why did William win at Hastings?

Sources that describe the battle are frequently complex. Very few sources exist that are contemporary, undoubtedly the most famous being the Bayeux Tapestry. Later authors who make use of earlier sources often interpolate (insert) new detail. Sometimes this is fabricated. Sometimes it is material copied from an earlier author whose work was known at the time but is now lost. This means that all sources must be considered carefully in order to assess their credentials – just because a source is not contemporary with the event it is describing does not mean that it is necessarily diminished in value.

Source Investigation. Why did William win at Hastings? Study Sources A–I.

1) Study Sources A–I. Each of these sources suggests a reason(s) for William's victory. Copy and complete the table below by using the sources. Try and select short quotations from the sources. Source A has been used as an exemplar.

	1) Mistakes and errors of Harold	2) Assets and advantages of William	3) Other, e.g. luck
Source A	Harold does not seem to have anticipated an attack	'William came upon Harold by surprise'.	God was on the side of the Normans; the English were sinners.
Source B			
Source C			
Source D			
Source E			
Source F			
Source G			
Source H			
Source I			

2) Use your findings from question 1) and your contextual knowledge to answer one of these questions:

   a) 'William won at Hastings because he was a better leader than Harold'. How far do you agree with this statement? Use Sources A–I and your own knowledge to explain your answer.

   b) 'William did not win at Hastings; Harold lost'. How far do you agree with this statement? Use Sources A–I and your own knowledge to explain your answer.

   c) What best explains why Harold lost at Hastings. Use Sources A–I and your own knowledge to explain your answer.

3) Study Sources A and G. To what extent does Source G support Source A? Explain your answer using details from each source.

4) Study Source D. How reliable do you consider this Source as a description of an aspect of the battle? Explain your answer.

Source A. *Anglo-Saxon Chronicle*. The Chronicle was first begun at the end of the ninth century. It is a contemporary record of events, written by monks in England.

[When King Harold was informed of the landing of William at Pevensey] he assembled a large army and came against him at the old apple tree [probably a reference to a tree on Senlac Hill]. But William came upon him by surprise before Harold's army was drawn up in battle formation. The French [i.e. the Normans] emerged as masters of the field, even as God granted it to them because of the sins of the people.

Source B. An artist's impression of a scene from the Bayeux Tapestry showing the burning of a house with a woman inside. (William did great damage to the territory around Pevensey in order to lure Harold out of

London.) The Tapestry was commissioned by Bishop Odo, the half-brother of William. It seems to have been produced in England in the early 1070s.

Source C. Song of the Battle of Hastings (the Carmen), attributed to Bishop Guy of Amiens and possibly written in 1067.

[In the midst of battle] William showed a furious countenance [fierce determination] to the Normans [who seemed prone to flight]. You fly from sheep, not men, and fear without cause; what you are doing is most shameful! The sea lies behind you: the sea-voyage back is formidable, wind and weather against you. It is hard to return home, hard and long the voyage; here no way of escape remains for you.

Source D. Norman William of Poitiers (1020–c.1090) wrote his *Deeds of William, Duke of Normandy and King of England* about 1075–77. In his youth he was a soldier and later became a priest. He was not involved in the invasion of 1066.

Realising that they could not without severe loss overcome an army massed so strongly in close formation, the Normans and their allies feigned flight and simulated a retreat, for they recalled that only a short while ago [in the battle] their flight had given them advantage. The English, thinking victory within their grasp, shouted with triumph, and heaping insults upon our men, threatened utterly to destroy them. Several thousand of them, as before, gave rapid pursuit to those whom they thought to be in flight; but the Normans suddenly wheeling around their horses surrounded them and cut down their pursuers so that not one was left alive. Twice was this trick employed with the utmost success. But Duke William excelled them all both in bravery and soldier-craft, so that one might esteem him as at least the equal of the most praised generals of ancient Greece and Rome.

Source E. Florence of Worcester. *The Chronicle of Chronicles* was composed by a monk in Worcester in the first decades of the twelfth century.

[When it was reported to Harold, who was in the north,] that William had landed at Pevensey, the King at once, and in great haste, marched with his army to London. Although he knew that some of the bravest Englishmen had been killed in the two former battles [Fulford Gate and Stamford Bridge], and that one half of his army had not yet arrived, he did not hesitate to advance [from London] with all speed into Sussex against his enemies. On Saturday 14th October, before a third of his army was in order for fighting, Harold joined battle with them nine miles from Hastings, where his foes had erected a castle.

Source F. Orderic Vitalis, *The Ecclesiastical History*. Vitalis (1075–1142) wrote his *History* between 1123 and 1141. He was born in England to a Norman father and an English mother. About the age of ten he entered a monastery in Normandy, where he remained for the rest of his life.

[Harold's mother] Gytha, who was much affected by the death of her son Tostig, and his other faithful friends, sought to dissuade Harold from engaging in battle with the Normans. Harold's brother, Earl Gyrth, thus addressed him: 'it is best, dearest brother, that your courage should be tempered by discretion. You are worn by the conflict with the Norwegians [Harald Hardrada and his allies] from which you are only just come, you are in eager haste to give battle to the Normans. Allow yourself, I pray you, some time for rest.'

Source G. William of Malmesbury. *Deeds of the Kings of the English*. William (d. c.1143) was a monk at Malmesbury Abbey in Wiltshire. He completed his *Deeds* in 1125. His father was a Norman and his mother English.

[Over time] the appetite for literature and religion had decayed for several years before the arrival of the Normans. The clergy, contented with a very slight degree of learning, could scarcely stammer out the words of prayer. The monks mocked the rule of their order by fine vestments [clothes], and the use of every kind of food. The nobility were given up to luxury and wantonness [indulged in pleasure]. Drinking in parties was a universal practice, in which the common people passed entire nights as well as days. The mistakes and errors that accompany drunkenness arose, so that engaging William, more with rashness and careless fury than military skill, the Anglo-Saxons doomed themselves and their country to servitude.

Source H. Master Wace, (d. c.1174) His chronicle of the Norman Conquest from the *Roman de Rou*. Wace was a Norman poet. He claimed that this work was commissioned by Henry II.

The Norman archers with their bows shot thickly upon the English; but they covered themselves with their shields, so that the arrows could not reach their bodies, nor do any mischief, however good their aim, or however well they shot. Then the Normans determined to shoot their arrows upwards into the air, so that they might fall on their enemies' heads, and strike their faces. The archers adopted this scheme, and shot up into the air towards the English; and the arrows in falling struck their heads and faces, and put out the eyes of many; and all feared to open their eyes, or leave their faces unguarded.

Source I. Henry of Huntingdon, *The History of the English*. Henry (c.1088– c.1157) was the son of a Norman father and an English woman. He was archdeacon of Huntingdon from 1118. He had completed his account of Hastings by 1130.

Twenty of the bravest knights also pledged their troth [made an oath of loyalty] to each other that they would cut through the English troops and capture the royal ensign [flag] called the standard. In this attack the greater part was slain, but the remainder, hacking away with their swords, captured the standard.

6) How did William impose his authority in the immediate aftermath of Hastings?

William remained at Hastings for about one week after his defeat of Harold, probably expecting during this time that he would receive the submission of the surviving English leaders. In fact, some of these latter, including leading men from the City of London, now moved to elect as king Edgar the Atheling. As such, William was clearly not yet deserving of the title of 'the Conqueror': for that title to be legitimate it was necessary for him to impose his authority throughout England. After all, there were perhaps only 7,000 Normans against an indigenous (native) population of some two million. It was thus essential that William enhance his authority. He realized that he must be crowned, sooner rather than later, and in a manner that advertised his authority to all. He thus resolved to march on London.

From Hastings William in fact did not move directly onto London, but marched instead on Dover and Canterbury, each of which submitted without resistance. After skirmishing with troops loyal to Edgar on the south end of London Bridge, William resolved to isolate the capital. He thus travelled west, allowing his army to pillage at will and terrifying all they encountered. This induced the submission of Winchester, significant because it was the ancient capital of England and held by Edith, the widow of Ethelred and the sister of Harold. Other submissions occurred when William reached Wallingford, including that of Archbishop Stigand; at Berkhamstead Earls Edwin and Morcar (the English earls who had failed to show up at Hastings), Archbishop Ealdred, and all the chief men of London submitted, including Edgar the Atheling. In what had been a brilliant military strategy, William had ensured that he was able to enter his new capital with relative ease. The way was now clear for him to be crowned.

Questions

1) Study Source A. Make a copy of Source A. Add further details to it using the paragraph above.

2) Study Sources B and C. What do Sources B and C suggest about William's attitude and approach to his new kingdom? Explain your answer.

Source A. Map showing the movements of William after Hastings.

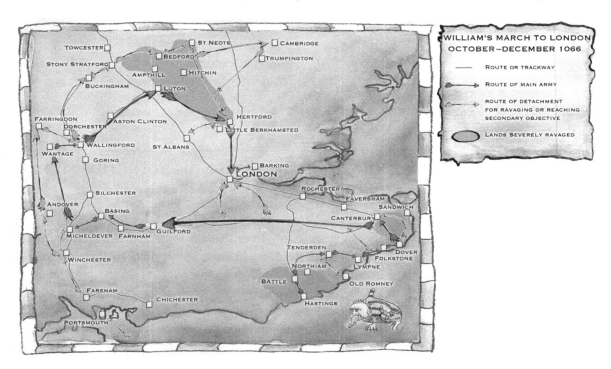

Source B. A writ issued by William in late 1066 or early 1067. It was written in English.

> William the King greets William, bishop of London, and Gosfrith, the port reeve, and all the burgesses of London. I wish you to know that I will abide by all the laws you were worthy of in the time of King Edward [the Confessor]. And I will that every child shall be his father's heir after his father's day (i.e. when his father dies). And I will not suffer any man to do you wrong. God preserve you.

Source C. Orderic Vitalis, *The Ecclesiastical History*. Vitalis (1075–1142) wrote his *History* between 1123 and 1141. He was born in England to a Norman father and an English mother. From about the age of 10 he entered the monastery in Normandy, where he remained for the rest of his life.

> [William's] passion for justice dominated the kingdom, encouraging others to follow his example. He attempted to learn some of the English language, so that he could understand the pleas of the conquered people without an interpreter but advancing age prevented him from acquiring such learning.
>
> The coronation of William by Archbishop Ealdred took place on Christmas Day 1066 in Westminster Abbey. When loud cheers from within the abbey perplexed and disturbed the guards outside, the latter suspected an uprising inspired by the English and set fire to nearby properties. One chronicler recorded that 'Only the bishops and a few clergy and monks remained, terrified, in the abbey, and with difficulty completed the crowning of the king who was trembling from head to foot.' It was an ominous beginning. Nonetheless, William, already Duke of Normandy, was henceforth also king of the English and as such was imbued with the mystical powers of that office.

Source Investigation. The coronation of William

1. Study Source A. This is a modern imagining of what the lost panel of the Bayeux Tapestry showing the crowning of William may have looked like. How far do you think it is a faithful representation of what we know took place? Explain your answer using your own knowledge and details in the source.

2. Study Source B. This is a modern artist's representation of the crowning of William. How does this differ from the representation of the crowning of William shown in Source A? How can you explain these differences?

3. 'A brilliant military strategy'. How far do you agree with this remark about William's actions between the battle at Hastings and his coronation? Explain your answer.

123

Source B. A modern artist's interpretation of the coronation of William I.

7) Exam practice and online resources

Questions in the style of Edexcel

a) 4 marks per question

i) Describe two features of a huscarl.

ii) Describe two features of a knight.

iii) Describe two features of William's coronation ceremony in December 1066.

b) 12 marks

Explain why there was a disputed succession to the throne when Edward the Confessor died. You may use the following in your answer:
- Edward
- Harold

You must also use information of your own.

c) 16 marks per question

i) 'The contender with the strongest claim to the throne after the death of Edward the Confessor was William'. How far do you agree? You may use the following in your answer:

- Duke William
- Edgar the Atheling

You must also use information of your own.

ii) 'The most important reason for the Norman victory at the Battle of Hastings was because of the leadership of Duke William'. How far do you agree? You may use the following in your answer:

- feigned retreat
- knights

You must also use information of your own.

Questions in the style of AQA

a) 8 marks

Study Source A. How convincing is this interpretation of the Battle of Hastings? Explain your answer using Interpretation A and your contextual knowledge.

Source A. A modern artist's impression of the Battle of Hastings.

b) 8 marks per question

i) Explain the causes and consequences of the Battles of Gate Fulford and Stamford Bridge.

ii) Explain why William won the Battle of Hastings.

c) 8 marks per question

i) Write an account of William's preparations for invading England, having learned of the death of Edward the Confessor in January 1066.

ii) Write an account detailing the actions taken by William in the period after the Battle of Hastings, concluding in December 1066.

Online Resources

Professor Nicholas Vincent, from UEA, explores the validity of the various claims of the pretenders to the English throne in 1066 https://www.uea.ac.uk/history/podcasts

Detailed narration of the entire Bayeux Tapestry, accompanied with illustrations http://www.angelfire.com/mb2/battle_hastings_1066/bayeux_tapestry/index.html

English Heritage 1066 site. Lots of interesting and useful pages http://www.english-heritage.org.uk/learn/1066-and-the-norman-conquest/

A very detailed site focussing on the year 1066 http://www.battle1066.com/intro.shtml

BBC Radio 4. Melvyn Bragg and guests discuss the Battle of Stamford Bridge http://www.bbc.co.uk/programmes/b011jvlt#in=collection:p01dh5yg

5 REBELLIONS OF 1067–71

Key Issues

Timeline

1067: Revolt of Edric the Wild; revolt of Eustace of Boulogne

1068: Resistance at Exeter; rebellion of Edwin and Morcar

1069: Rebellion in the north; Danish invasion

1069–70: Harrying of the north

1070–71: Invasion of King Estrithson; rebellion of Hereward the Wake; English bishops purged

1072: William invades Scotland; Treaty of Abernethy

Overview

The phrase 'the' Norman Conquest is, in fact, misleading, because there exists no single transformative event that marks the moment from which the whole of England became Norman, and no overnight change overnight from Anglo-Saxon to Norman England. Instead, the imposition of Norman authority in England took place incrementally (bit by bit) over a number of years. One reason for this was because William had to spend much time and energy from 1066 suppressing a series of rebellions, some of which were led by disaffected Anglo-Saxons and others of which were led by Scandinavians. Historians generally agree that William had weathered the worst of these rebellions by the early 1070s, though Norman rule arguably was not secure until as late as the 1080s. This chapter examines the rebellions that William faced from 1067 through to the early 1070s, and identifies reasons why they failed.

1) Why did William face rebellions in England during 1067–71?

William, as both duke of Normandy and king of England, ruled two large dominions divided by the English Channel. Therefore his first priority was to undertake a number of actions to secure his control over the English Crown so that he could return to Normandy as and when required. He had quickly ordered the building of a castle in London (the future 'Tower', see Source F, p. 143) and other key towns to create garrisons under his firm control in the main centres of government. He allocated lands deemed strategically important, such as those guarding the entrances to the main river estuaries in East Anglia, to his most trusted friends. In addition, when William returned to Normandy in March 1067 for the first time since arriving in England, he appointed trusted agents William fitz Osbern and Bishop Odo to act as regents during his absence. He also took with him to Normandy as hostages leading members of the English nobility, including Archbishop Stigand, Earls Edwin and Morcar and Edgar the Atheling. This extraordinary party was paraded around and gawped at by astonished members of the Norman court. Meanwhile, accessible parts of England were despoiled, allowing huge amounts of treasure to be sent back to Normandy as early as January 1067 and, in effect, buying support.

This treatment of leading Englishmen, coupled with the ongoing despoliation of English lands, was not a programme designed to win hearts and minds: on 6 December 1067 William was forced to return from Normandy to deal with rebellion in England.

Questions

1) What strategic problems do you think William encountered as a ruler of a cross-Channel dominion? Explain your answer.

2) Study Sources A and B. Use these sources and your own knowledge to explain why William faced resistance despite his victory at Hastings.

3) Study Sources B and C. Use these sources and your own knowledge to assess the scale of the resistance to William. Explain your answer.

4) Study Sources A and C. Use these sources and your own knowledge to explain how William tried to deal with resistance in the early months of his rule as king of England.

Source A: *The Anglo-Saxon Chronicle.* The *Chronicle* was first begun at the end of the ninth century. It is a contemporary record of events, written by monks in England.

After the battle [of Hastings], Archbishop Ealdred and the citizens of London wanted to have Prince Edgar as king, as was his proper due. [See the family tree on p. 84.] And Edwin and Morcar promised him that they would fight on his side. William waited at Hastings to see if submission would be made to him. But when he understood that no one intended to come to him, he went inland with all his army that was left to him and ravaged [destroyed] all the region that he overran until he reached Berkhamstead. There he was met by Archbishop Ealdred and Prince Edgar, and Earls Edwin and Morcar, and all the chief men from London. And they submitted out of necessity after most damage had been done – and it was a great piece of folly that they had not submitted earlier. And they gave hostages and swore oaths to William; and he promised that he would be a gracious liege lord: and yet in the meantime he ravaged all that he had overrun. Then on Christmas Day 1066, Archbishop Ealdred crowned him at Westminster. [William] then laid taxes on people very severely. [When he went to Normandy, his regents] stayed behind and built castles far and wide throughout this country, and distressed the common folk. From this time on it grew much worse. May the end be good when God wills!

Source B. Orderic Vitalis, *The Ecclesiastical History.* Vitalis (1075–1142) wrote his *History* between 1123 and 1141. He was born in England to a Norman father and an English mother. From about the age of ten he entered the monastery in Normandy, where he remained for the rest of his life.

After large numbers of the leading men of England and Wales had met together, a general outcry arose against the injustice and tyranny which the Normans and their comrades-in-arms had inflicted on the English. These leading men sent messengers into every corner of Albion [England] to incite men openly and secretly against the enemy. All were ready to conspire [plot] together to recover their former liberty, and bind themselves by serious oaths against the Normans. In the regions north of the River Humber violent disturbances broke out. The rebels prepared to defend themselves in woods, marshes, and creeks, and in some cities.

Source C. The Norman William of Poitiers (1020–c.1090) wrote his *Deeds of William, Duke of Normandy and King of England* around 1071. In his youth he was a soldier and later became a priest. He was not involved in the invasion of 1066.

> Neither benefits nor fear could sufficiently force the English to prefer peace and quiet to changes and revolts. They had not the courage to rise in arms openly, but dealt in vile conspiracies in different regions, to see if by deceit they could succeed in inflicting damage. They repeatedly sent envoys [i.e. representatives] to the Danes or some other people from whom they might hope for help.

2) What were the character, location and frequency of the rebellions against William during 1067–71?

From the end of 1067 until 1072 William was mostly resident in his new kingdom, primarily engaged in suppressing rebellions and responding to invasions, threatened and real.

Questions

1) Study Source A and read carefully the details of each of the rebellions in Information Boxes 1)–8). Draw your own version of this map and annotate it appropriately to show the rebellions that William faced in 1067–71.

2) What does the scale and frequency of the rebellions shown on your map suggest about support for the Norman regime? Explain your answer.

Source A Map showing William's movements, 1067–72.

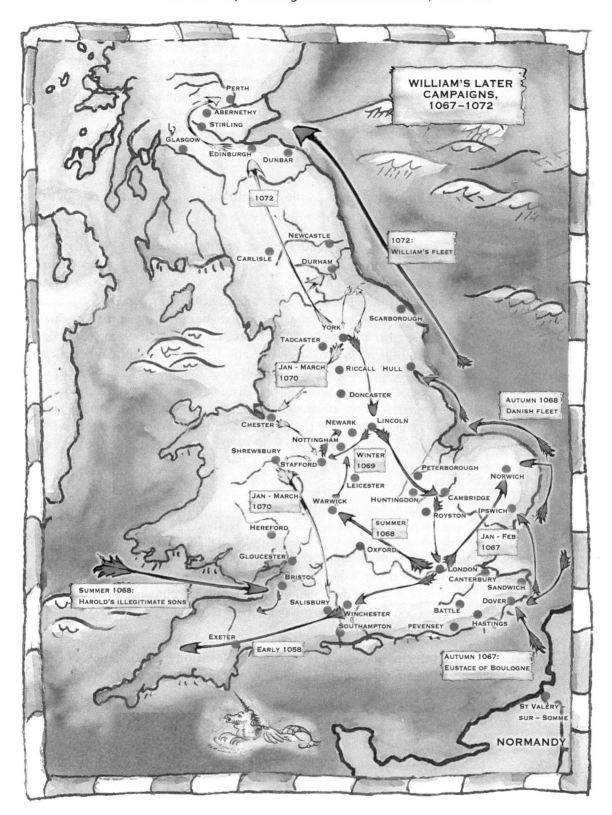

Information Box 1. 1067, Herefordshire: the revolt of Edric the Wild

Edric held land in Herefordshire, but most of his estates lay in Shropshire. He was one of the richest lay **magnates** below the rank of earl. Whilst William was absent in Normandy Edric raised a revolt in Herefordshire. He called to his assistance the Welsh princes, Bleddyn and Riwallon. They caused much devastation but failed to gain control of Herefordshire. Having obtained booty (valuable items), they melted back into their territories, but reappeared during the disturbances of 1069. (See below.)

Information Box 2. 1067, Kent: the revolt of Eustace, Count of Boulogne

Eustace's family had a traditional hostility towards the Norman dukes, but in 1066 he had joined William in the Conquest, even featuring prominently on the Bayeux Tapestry, where he is shown holding a banner in the thick of the fight and, incidentally, by so doing, immortalizing his splendid moustache! He had been married to a daughter of Ethelred the Unready. Eustace became briefly estranged (i.e. at odds) from William in 1067, and whilst the latter was in Normandy, the count crossed the Channel with a substantial number of knights. With both regents occupied north of the Thames, Eustace occupied the town of Dover. However, an attempt to take the newly built castle led to the rebel force being decimated, and Eustace made his escape across the Channel. He was quickly reconciled with William and was restored to the extensive estates that he had received directly after the Conquest.

Information Box 3. 1068, early spring, resistance by the city of Exeter

The city had refused to submit to the new regime, perhaps inspired by the presence of Harold's mother, Gytha, and had sought to form a league of resistance among the neighbouring towns. It held out against William for 18 days before surrendering, encouraging other towns such as Gloucester and Bristol to do the same.

Information Box 4. 1068, summer, invasion from Ireland led by three illegitimate sons of Harold

The Anglo-Saxon Chronicle states that they came with 'a naval force into the mouth of the Avon and ravaged all over the district'. However, they mobilized little support. Even Bristol, only recently having submitted [to William], 'fought against them fiercely'. Driven back, they sailed to Somerset where they disappear from the pages of history.

Information Box 5. 1068, rebellion of Edwin and Morcar

In 1068, local resistance in the north was forming around Morcar. Having been released from his role as hostage in the Conqueror's triumphal procession through Normandy, he seems to have been intent upon a full restoration of his position as Earl of Northumbria. He was joined by his brother Edwin, motivated at least in part, it seems, by William's failure to honour his promise of his daughter's hand in marriage and in part by the appointment of Roger de Montgomery as Earl of Shrewsbury (thus undermining Edwin's influence in that region). Ominously for William, it was at this point that Edgar the Atheling departed from court and took refuge with King Malcolm of Scotland. These northern rebels then met with the Welsh princes in an attempt to incite a general rebellion.

Information Box 6. 1069, January to April, rebellion of the north

Unable to trust either Edwin or Morcar, William had appointed as Earl of Northumbria a Norman, Robert de Commines, and sent him to impose authority in the north. However, upon his arrival at Durham on 28 January 1069, Robert was attacked in the street and then burned to death in the bishop's house where he was lodging. Of the perhaps 900-strong body of knights that had accompanied Robert, all but two of them were slaughtered. This inspired copy-cat rebellions, especially in York, where rebels laid siege to the new castle. (It is worthy of note that neither Edwin nor Morcar played a role in the rebellions of 1069.)

Information Box 7. 1069, summer, Danish invasion

In the summer of 1069 a Danish fleet consisting of some 240 ships sought to make a landing at various ports on the east and the south coast, including Dover and Sandwich. The king of Denmark, Swein Estrithson (r. 1047–76), did not participate personally in this invasion, but was motivated in part to send such a force to increase the pressure upon the Norman regime but also by the prospect of making real his claim to the throne, established by the fact that he was the son of King Cnut's sister and the cousin of King Harthacnut. The Danes eventually landed on the banks of the Humber, where they joined with rebels led by Edgar the Atheling; Gospatric, Earl of Northumbria; and Waltheof, son of Earl Siward of Northumbria. They captured York on 20 September. Thereafter, many of this Danish force crossed the Humber into North Lincolnshire and found themselves welcomed – after all, this was part of the old area of Scandinavian influence, the Danelaw. Meanwhile, minor revolts occurred in places as far distant from Yorkshire as Dorset and Somerset, and across the Pennines, in Staffordshire and South Cheshire. Once again, the Scottish king lent his support to the rebels.

Information Box 8. 1070–71, invasion of King Estrithson and the rebellion of Hereward

In this year the king of Denmark arrived in person and sent an element of his army to the Isle of Ely in Cambridgeshire (the Isle was an inland island surrounded by marshes), to join with the one remaining pocket of English resistance: a rebel group led by the English thegn, Hereward (latterly awarded the epithet – nickname – of 'the Wake', meaning 'the watchful'). After a period of time the Danes withdrew, but Hereward was sustained by the arrival of Morcar. (His brother Edwin was murdered at some point before Morcar's arrival.) William eventually led a successful assault on the Isle of Ely, but not before employing a witch to cast down her spells on the rebels and display her bare backside from the top of a wooden tower. Morcar was captured and imprisoned; Hereward fled and disappeared from the record. The witch was burned to death in the tower.

Supplementary information to box 8. Maps showing the location of the Isle of Ely and the same at the time of Hereward the Wake.

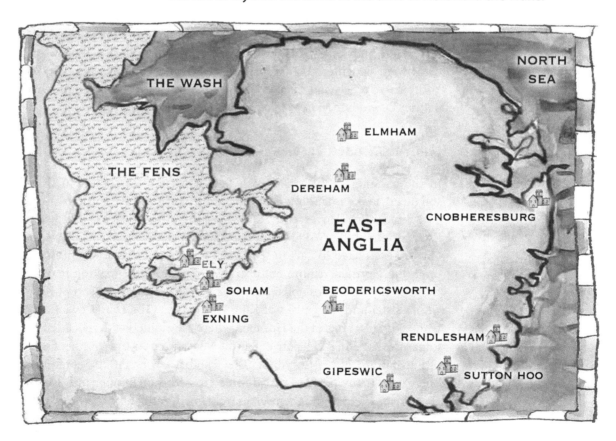

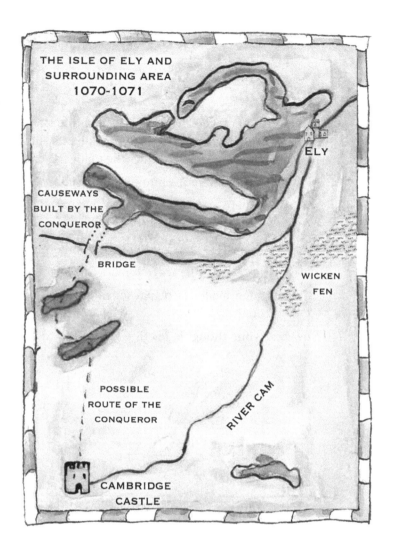

3) How serious were the threats posed to William's authority by the rebellions of 1067–71?

Questions

1) For each of the rebellions described in Information Boxes 1–8 above assess the scale of the threat it posed to William's authority. When judging each rebellion you should consider the following criteria:

   - How large were the numbers involved?
   - Was there any participation by magnates? If so, on what scale?
   - Does the rebellion have any significant geographical extent?
   - Does the rebellion have links with other rebellions?
   - Is there any evidence of foreign involvement/support?
   - Is there evidence of participation of an alternative claimant to the throne?

Now plot your thoughts on this graph, awarding each of the rebellions a mark /10:

Names and dates of rebellions

2) 'At no point in the period 1067–71 was William's authority in danger'. How far do you agree? Explain your answer. (Use your completed graph to inform your answer.)

3) Read Source A, an interpretation by D.C. Douglas about the rebellion of 1069. How far do you agree with this interpretation of events? Explain your answer using your contextual knowledge.

Source A. From *William the Conqueror* by D. C. Douglas (1964). Here Douglas comments upon the rebellion of 1069.

> The whole Norman venture in England had been placed in peril, for at last the resistance to William was assuming a coherence which it had hitherto lacked. A strong Scandinavian force was at large in England, and it was supported by a considerable army led by powerful Saxon magnates. The centre of the crisis was in the north. Yorkshire had been lost, and beyond Yorkshire, north of the River Tees, there was whirling chaos, in which was emerging the authority of Malcolm, king of Scotland. The Scottish king had

in fact now thrown in his lot with William's opponents in England, and it was probably about this time that, by one of the most influential marriages in English history, he allied himself to Margaret, the sister of Edgar the Atheling. The possibilities latent [showing potential but not explicit] in the developing situation were in fact incalculable, and in the autumn of 1069 it must have seemed possible that the Scandinavian kingdom might once more be established in northern England, or even a realm created for Edgar the Atheling, buttressed by the support of Malcolm and Swein, perhaps even to be sanctioned [made legitimate] with a separate coronation by the Archbishop of York.

4) How did William overcome the rebellions of 1067–71?

The conquest of England was achieved over a period of time and by a number of actions and processes, including especially

the building of castles;

the creation of 'marcher' earldoms; and
William's energy, resolve and military success.

Rebellion was also overcome by William's policy of rewarding his followers with land (discussed on pp. 62–63) and with important positions in the state and church. This meant that the Normans had an interest in ensuring that the Conquest was enduring because they were, in effect, stakeholders in the process.

i) Castles

Many of the earliest Norman castles were ringworks – an oval enclosure with bank and ditch. However, motte and bailey castles soon outnumbered ringworks. As the name suggests, motte and bailey castles had two distinct parts. The motte was a mound of earth – usually man-made – and ranged in height from three to thirty metres. Upon the flattened top of the motte the Normans placed a wooden fort or tower called a keep. The keep was encircled by a wooden fence placed around the perimeter at the top of the motte. The excavation of earth meant that the base of the motte was protected by a ditch. The bailey was an area found at the base of the motte and was of larger scale than the motte. Like the keep it was protected by a man-made ditch and a wooden fence. The bailey provided an area in which accommodation was built, for men as well as for storage of food, goods and animals.

As the Normans became more secure, the wooden features of motte and bailey castles were replaced with stone, though the more important ones seem to have been built out of stone in the first instance. The Tower of London, built c.1070, is perhaps the best example of an early stone-built castle, and to this day inspires respect. Nothing quite like it had ever been seen in England before. The building was immense, at 36m x 32.5m (118 x 106ft) across, and on the south side where the ground is lowest, 27.5m (90ft) tall. The Tower dominated the skyline for miles around. The looming presence of castles must have had a psychological as well as physical impact on the conquered English.

Castles were planted in leading administrative centres and in the main areas of rebellion. In York two castles within sight of each other appear to have been established in a matter of months in 1069, the second castle built within the space of eight days. By 1100 it is estimated that there were perhaps as many as 500 castles in England, built in villages and towns. The sites for many early castles erected inside existing towns were cleared through the destruction of large numbers of houses, as recorded by Domesday Book. For instance, at Lincoln 160 houses were destroyed, at Norwich 98 houses and at Shrewsbury 51 houses. Quickly erected, these early castles not only acted as a formidable physical presence of the Norman regime, but they also provided a fortified centre of administration and a base from which garrisons could operate to take swift action against English rebels.

Whilst there is no doubt that castles were protective structures with a military function, recent research has cautioned against the notion that this wholly explains the building of castles. This research has pointed out that the location and architecture of many early castles were not dominated by military considerations. The majority of castles were built in river valleys, which meant that their defensive capacity was compromised because they were often overlooked by higher ground. Moreover, the military features of castle architecture became more prominent in the twelfth and thirteenth centuries, and were less pronounced in castles built in the 1070s and 1080s. These findings suggest that the main priority for those who built castles in the early years of Norman rule was to display their status and rank, to announce their arrival, and to underline their governance of England and Wales in an impressive and formidable manner, rather than to subjugate by force a hostile population. In short, there is not necessarily a straightforward equation between the building of castles and military strategy during the period of the Norman Conquest.

Questions

1) Study Source A. What part of the castle-building process is shown in this scene from the Bayeux Tapestry?

2) Study Source B. Draw your own version of this illustration and add labels identifying each of the following:

   - keep
   - motte
   - bailey
   - ditch
   - defensive fences

3) Study Source C. In what ways is this second-generation Norman castle a) similar to and b) different from the artist's representation shown in Source A?

4) Study Sources D, E and F. Use Sources D, E and F and your own knowledge to explain why the English could 'resist only weakly' once William had built motte and bailey castles.

5) Task: Historians evaluate evidence by studying it in context, that is, in the circumstances/setting in which the evidence is located. Study Source G. i) Identify the ways in which Liddiard uses contextual analysis to cast doubt on Orderic Vitalis's judgement about the impact of castles upon the English. ii) How compelling do you consider Liddiard's evaluation of Vitalis? Explain your answer.

Source A. Modern artist's impression of a scene from the Bayeux Tapestry.

Source B. A modern artist's impression of a motte and bailey castle.

Source C. A modern artist's impression of Pickering castle in Yorkshire. This was originally built by William I in 1069–70. It was modified and improved at the beginning of the thirteenth century.

Source D. Orderic Vitalis, *The Ecclesiastical History*. Vitalis (1075–1142) wrote his *History* between 1123 and 1141. He was born in England to a Norman father and an English mother. About the age of ten he entered a monastery in Normandy, where he remained for the rest of his life.

> To deal with the danger of rebellion, King William rode to the furthest parts of his kingdom. He fortified the right sort of places against enemy attacks. The Normans called these fortifications 'castles', and hardly anyone in England had known about them before. The English were brave and they loved fighting, but now they could resist only weakly.

Source E. *Anglo-Saxon Chronicle*. The *Chronicle* was first begun at the end of the ninth century. It is a contemporary record of events, written by monks in England.

> [The Normans] sorely burdened the unhappy people of the country with forced labour on the castles. And when the castles were made they filled them with devils and wicked men.

Source F. The Tower of London (probably built in the 1070s).

Source G. From *Castles in Context*, R. Liddiard (2005)

> In his *Ecclesiastical History* of c.1125, Orderic Vitalis famously remarked that 'the fortifications called castles by the Normans were scarcely known in

the English provinces, and so the English – in spite of their courage and love of fighting – could only put up weak resistance to their enemies'. Orderic's apparently clear statement is not without its ambiguities [lack of clarity]. His comments on the almost complete absence of castles appear in a part of his narrative specifically concerning William the Conqueror's campaign through the Midlands in 1068, and applying his reasoning to the national situation is problematic. It is also possible that Orderic was simply following an earlier account of events given by William of Poitiers in the *Gesta Guillelmi*, in which case these remarks should be treated within the context of a piece of writing intended to praise the martial [warlike] virtues of William the Conqueror. Orderic himself was of mixed Anglo-Norman parentage and his family connections with Shropshire (a shire ravaged (i.e. destroyed) by William in 1069) may have led him to offer a simplistic explanation for the events of these years. Moreover by the time Orderic was writing (c.1125) there had been a rapid increase in the number of castles built on both sides of the Channel. From the standpoint of the twelfth century when, indeed, large masonry castles were more common features in the landscape, it may well have been reasonable to assume that an absence of castles had been a major factor in the English defeat.

ii) The creation of the 'marcher' earldoms

The frontier zone between the English kingdom and Wales – an area known as the Welsh March – was territory which English rulers looked to subdue or subject to their authority. The kings of England relied upon the barons of the March both to defend the kingdom from Welsh incursions and to provide a secure base from which assaults could be launched on Wales. William carved out three great new 'marcher' earldoms of Chester, Shrewsbury and Hereford and staffed them with his trusted lieutenants Hugh d'Avranches, Roger de Montgomery and William fitz Osbern respectively. These men were – and were expected to be – hard, ruthless and effective, with the ability to think on their feet.

In order to fulfil their roles the marcher barons had to dominate the borderlands utterly. To this end they held significant powers derived from the king: the right to exercise justice, to make war and to build castles. Indeed, the creation of the Marcher earldoms led to a castle-building programme that established the densest concentration of motte and bailey castles in Britain. The castle at Chepstow, like the Tower of London, is particularly notable for being constructed out of stone as opposed to the earthwork and timber structures elsewhere.

William did not establish northern marches along the border with Scotland in the same way that he had with Wales even though the northern kingdom arguably posed in a number of ways a greater threat than Wales: it was ruled over by a single king, it regularly acted as the bolthole for dissident English elements and its southern borders were alarmingly ill-defined. Instead, in the autumn of 1072 William determined upon a remarkable combined sea and land invasion of Scotland in an attempt to bring that northern territory to heel once and for all. Although the campaign did not result in battle, it was sufficient to scare King Malcolm to the negotiating table. The resulting Peace of Abernethy (1072) ensured that Malcolm formally recognized the new regime in England, apparently giving his son Duncan as hostage. The Scottish King also expelled Edgar the Atheling.

Question

1) Study Sources A and B. Use these sources and your own knowledge to explain how William contained the threat from the Welsh.

Source A. Map showing the distribution of early Norman motte and bailey castles.

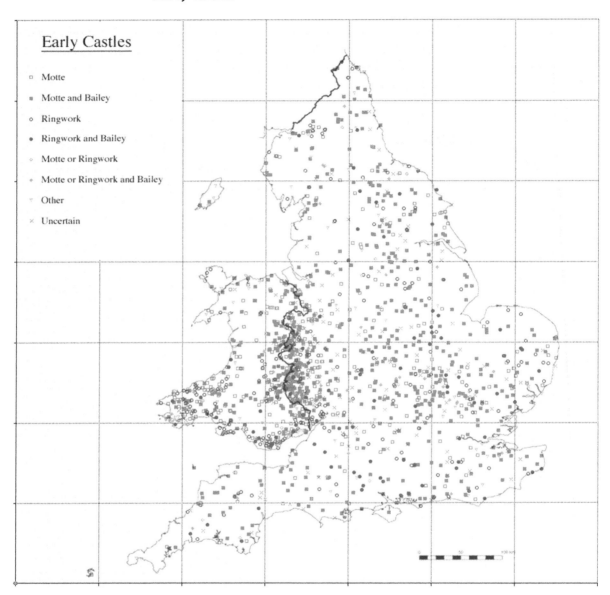

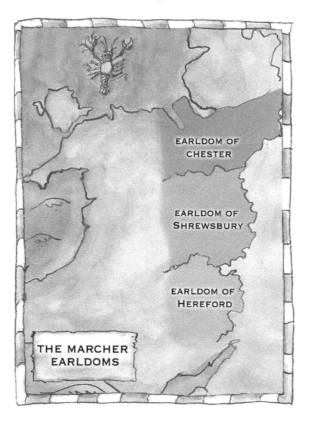

Source B. Map showing the Marcher earldoms.

EARLDOM OF
CHESTER

EARLDOM OF
SHREWSBURY

EARLDOM OF
HEREFORD

THE MARCHER
EARLDOMS

iii) William's energy, resolve and military success

The speed, energy, resolve and downright battle hardness of William are characteristics that help explain his success. For instance, he frequently led campaigns in person, from the assault upon the city of Exeter in 1068 to the attack upon the Isle of Ely in 1071. The first nine months of 1068 in particular witnessed a breathless series of campaigns over large tracts of England stretching from Exeter to York, followed by a determined winter march over the Pennines in order to put down a rebellion in Chester. William was everywhere. To contemporaries, it must have seemed that, like his great-grandson Henry II, he was able to fly.

William was also certainly capable of great acts of state and asserted his authority by instituting thrice yearly crown-wearing ceremonies. Most memorably, after suppressing York for a third time, William sent to Winchester for his crown in order to hold a crown-wearing at Christmas 1069 in the then smouldering remains of York cathedral. He was pragmatic also, choosing simply to pay off the Danes in order to send them home in 1069 and again in 1071.

The most dramatic explanation for William overcoming threats to his authority is perhaps because of his systematic devastation of rebel territories, evidenced most compellingly by his actions in the north over the winter of

1069–70, the so-called '**harrying** of the north'. (See Key Issue 5.) The objective was to make the territory uninhabitable and thus unable to support further rebellion, as well as to instil raw terror.

Questions

1) Study Source A. Use Source A and your own knowledge to describe the main ways in which William asserted his authority, other than through the building of motte and bailey castles.

Source A. An illustrated manuscript showing William I undergoing a crowning ceremony as depicted in an illustration of Matthew Paris's (c.1200–59) *Flores Historiarum*.

5) What was the impact of the 'harrying of the north'?

As we saw on page 135, one of the biggest threats to William's authority occurred in 1069 when various rebel groups combined to capture York. William's response was brutal. It is known as the 'harrying of the north'. As recorded in Domesday Book, 16 years after the harrying, Yorkshire may still have contained only 25 per cent of the population and plough teams of 1066, some 80,000 oxen and 150,000 people fewer than had been there on the day that King Edward 'was alive and dead'.

Source Investigation. 'Harrying of the north'. Study Sources A–E.

1) Using details contained in Sources A–E, and your own knowledge, explain why William's actions in the north in 1069–70 are known as the 'harrying of the north'.

2) Which one of these sources do you consider most useful for an historian investigating the 'harrying of the north'? Explain your answer.

3) 'The main explanation for William overcoming threats to his authority in the period 1067–71 is because of his use of castles'. How far do you agree? (Think about the strengths of William and the weaknesses of his opponents.)

> **Source A. Orderic Vitalis, *The Ecclesiastical History*. Vitalis (1075–1142) wrote his *History* between 1123 and 1141. He was born in England to a Norman father and an English mother. From about the age of ten he entered the monastery in Normandy, where he remained for the rest of his life.**
>
> Nowhere else [in the country] had William shown such cruelty. Shamefully he succumbed to this vice, for he made no effort to restrain his fury and punished the innocent with the guilty. In his anger he commanded that all crops and herds, chattels and food of every kind should be brought together and burned to ashes with consuming fire, so that the whole region north of the Humber might be stripped of all means of sustenance. In consequence so serious a scarcity was felt in England, and so terrible a famine fell upon the humble and defenceless populace, that more than 100,000 Christian folk of both sexes, young and old alike, perished of hunger. My narrative has frequently had occasion to praise William, but for this act which condemned the innocent and the guilty alike to die by slow starvation I cannot commend him.
>
> **Source B. Symeon of Durham, *History of the Kings*. Symeon (d. c.1129) was a monk in Durham, writing in the early twelfth century. (Durham is an important city in the north of England.)**
>
> So great a famine prevailed that men, compelled by hunger, devoured human flesh, that of horses, dogs, and cats, and whatever custom abhors [hates]; others sold themselves to perpetual slavery, so that they might in any way preserve their wretched existence; others, while about to go into exile from their country, fell down in the middle of their journey and there they died. It was horrific to behold human corpses decaying in the houses, the streets, and the roads, swarming with worms, while they were consuming in corruption with an abominable stench. For no one was left to bury them in the earth, all being cut off either by the sword or by famine. Meanwhile, the land being thus deprived of any one to cultivate it for nine years, an extensive solitude prevailed all around. There was no village inhabited between

149

York and Durham; they became lurking places to wild beasts and robbers, and were a great dread to travellers.

Source C. William of Malmesbury (d. 1143c.) was a monk at Malmesbury Abbey in Wiltshire. He completed his *Deeds of the Kings of the English* in 1125.

[Malcolm King of the Scots] ravaged the neighbouring provinces of England with robbery and arson, not that he thought it would forward Edgar's hopes of becoming king, but to annoy William and make him angry at the sight of his own lands exposed to Scottish forays. William therefore got together a force of infantry and knights and made for the northern parts of the island. First he accepted the surrender of the metropolitan city, which was held tenaciously by English with Danes and Scots, after exhausting the citizens by a lengthy famine. He also routed a very large enemy force which had gathered to aid the besieged, in a massive and severe conflict, a victory far from bloodless, for he lost many of his own men. He then gave orders for the towns and fields of the whole region to be devastated, and the fruit and grain to be ruined by fire or water, especially near the sea, partly because of his recent anger, but also since a rumour had spread that Cnut King of the Danes, son of Swein, was approaching, the purpose of this order being to leave nothing near the seashore which a raiding pirate could find and carry off if he had to make a rapid return home, or use for food if he thought he could stay longer.

The resources of a province [the north], once flourishing, and the nurse of tyrants, were cut off by fire, slaughter and devastation; the ground, for more than sixty miles, totally uncultivated and unproductive, remains bare even to the present day. Should any stranger now see it, he laments over the once magnificent cities! The towers threatening heaven itself with their loftiness; the fields abundant in pasturage and watered with rivers: and if any ancient remains, he knows it no longer.

Source D. Map showing places in the north of England mentioned in Domesday Book as 'waste' (i.e. places that had been devastated/laid waste).

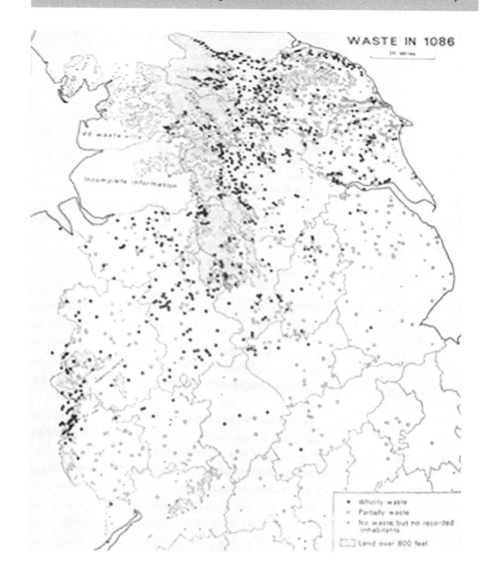

WASTE IN 1086

Wholly waste
Partially waste
No waste, but no recorded inhabitants
Land over 800 feet

Source E. Orderic Vitalis, *The Ecclesiastical History*. Vitalis (1075–1142) wrote his History between 1123 and 1141. He was born in England to a Norman father and an English mother. From about the age of ten he entered the monastery in Normandy, where he remained for the rest of his life. (In his History, Orderic presented William giving a speech from his deathbed.)

I caused the death of thousands by starvation and war, especially in Yorkshire. In a mad fury I descended on the English of the north like a raging lion, and ordered that their homes and crops and all their equipment and furnishings should be burnt at once and their great flocks and herds of sheep and cattle slaughtered everywhere. So I chastised a great multitude of men and women with the lash of starvation and, alas! was the cruel murderer of many thousands, both young and old.

Question

i) Study Source A. How far do you agree with Douglas's interpretation of the harrying of the north? Explain your answer.

Source A. *William the Conqueror* by D. C. Douglas. (1964) Here Douglas comments upon the 'harrying of the north'.

King William's campaign of 1069–70 must rank as one of the outstanding military achievements of the age, and it was to prove decisive in ensuring that the Norman domination of England would endure. Nonetheless, the cost of that achievement and its consequences deserve note in any estimate of the Norman impact upon England, and of the character of William the Conqueror. An eleventh-century campaign was inevitably brutal, but the methods here displayed were widely regarded as exceptional and beyond excuse.

6) Exam practice and online resources

Questions in the style of Edexcel

a) 4 marks per question

i) Describe two features of a Norman castle.

ii) Describe two features of the 'harrying' of the north.

b) 12 marks per question

i) Explain why William faced rebellions in England, 1067–1072. You may use the following in your answer:

- the continued existence of claimants to the throne such as Edgar the Atheling
- hostages

You must also use information of your own.

ii) Explain why William overcame the rebellions that he faced in England, 1067–1072. You may use the following in your answer:

- motte and bailey castles
- the character of William's rule in England

You must also use information of your own.

c) 16 marks

'The most important reason why William was able to overcome the rebellions that he faced in England in 1067–1071 was because of the building of motte and bailey castles'. How far do you agree? You may use the following in your answer:

- Tower of London
- William's direct actions, such as crown-wearing ceremonies

You must also use information of your own.

Questions in the style of AQA

a) 8 marks per question

i) Study Source A. How convincing is this interpretation of the construction and style of a Norman castle. Explain your answer using Interpretation A and your contextual knowledge.

Source A. An artistic impression of the building of a Norman castle – Pickering – in the twelfth century.

ii) Study Source B. How convincing is this interpretation of the 'harrying' of the north? Explain your answer using Interpretation B and your contextual knowledge.

Source B. A modern artist's representation of the 'harrying' of the north.

iii) Study Source C. How convincing is this interpretation of the impact of castles during the reign of William the Conqueror? Explain your answer using Interpretation B and your contextual knowledge.

Source C. *The Medieval Castle in England and Wales*, N. J. G. Pounds.

> It is impossible to exaggerate the role of castles in the Norman Conquest of this country. The castle became the instrument whereby the Conqueror fastened his grip on England.

iv) Study Source D. How convincing is this interpretation of the building of castles during the reign of William the Conqueror? Explain your answer using Interpretation B and your contextual knowledge.

Source D. *Castles in Context*, R. Liddiard, pp. 23–34

> The overall distribution of castles has sometimes been explained by reference to strategic military planning. [But] such ideas do not bear close examination. Across England and Wales, castles were built for a variety of social and economic reasons, rather than as a response to one immediate threat that might necessitate a programme of defensive works. Even where high densities exist, for example in the Welsh borders, the evidence points to successive waves of castle construction rather than an organized system of border defence.

b) 8 marks per question

i) Explain why William faced so many rebellions during the years 1067–1071.

ii) Explain why William was able to overcome the rebellions that he faced during the years 1067–1071.

c) 8 marks per question

i) Write an account of the revolt of Earls Edwin and Morcar.

ii) Write an account of the rebellion of Hereward the Wake.

iii) Write an account of the causes and consequences of the 'harrying' of the north.

Online Resources

Lucy Martin from UEA examines the castle, its role and function. https://www.uea.ac.uk/history/podcasts.

Illustrated list of surviving castles in England http://www.geograph.org.uk/article/Castles-England.

'All the noblest and bravest of the English who still resisted William gathered to Hereward and they made their camp in the Isle of Ely'. H. E. *Marshall's Our Island Story: A Child's History of England*, published 1905. Read her view of Hereward the Wake as a freedom fighter. http://www.mainlesson.com/display.php?author=marshall&book=island&story=hereward.

The impact of the 'harrying' of the north http://stokesleyheritage.wikidot.com/the-harrying-of-the-north.

Site dedicated to the study and promotion of British castles http://www.castles-of-britain.com/.

6 REBELLIONS OF 1073–88

Key Issues

Timeline

1075: Revolt of the Earls

1078–80: Revolt of Robert Curthose

c.1082: Arrest of Bishop Odo

1085: Rumours of Scandinavian invasion; death of Gregory VII; Domesday Book commissioned by William the Conqueror

Overview

From 1073 until 1085 William was mostly resident in Normandy, dealing in the first instance with a revolt in Maine and an increasingly hostile Flanders, where Edgar the Atheling had found asylum after his expulsion from Scotland according to the Peace of Abernethy. Of greatest concern to William from the early 1070s was the emergence of King Philip I of France from his **minority**. Aged 18 in 1070, Philip's essential ambition over the next 20 years was to break Normandy, conducted in alliance with Flanders and Anjou. On two particular occasions – 1075 and 1085 – this had dramatic consequences for England. This chapter examines those consequences, along with William's relations with this eldest son, Robert, and his half-brother, Odo.

1) What was the background to the Revolt of the Earls?

King Malcolm of Scotland did little to observe the terms of the Peace of Abernethy (1072) (See p. 145). Scottish raids into Northumbria continued, and in 1074 Edgar the Atheling, whose sister Margaret was married to Malcolm, was welcomed back to Scotland from his exile in Flanders. It thus seemed as though Edgar might again act as a rallying point for all the enemies of the Anglo-Norman kingdom. Philip, king of France, was an enemy of William and eager to stir up opposition in William's dominions, and so he gave Edgar the important castle of Montreuil-sur-Mer, which was the main French gateway to the English Channel. But a chance sequence of events resulted in the disappearance of this threat. First, shipwreck prevented Edgar from reaching Montreuil, so he returned to Scotland. Then, Edgar decided to submit to William, effectively relinquishing any claim to the throne, for which he was accepted at his court.

With Edgar thus neutralized, Philip sought another way to destabilize William, and developments in Brittany now presented circumstances that could be made highly dangerous to Normandy. The outcome is known as the Revolt of the Earls.

Questions

1) Study Source A. Use Source A and your own knowledge to explain how Edgar the Atheling posed a threat to William in the early 1070s.

2) How great was the threat to William posed by Edgar the Atheling? Explain your answer.

Source A. Map showing the location of Montreuil-sur-Mer.

COMTÉ
DE
FLANDRE

MONTREUIL
SUR - MER

DUCHÉ
DE
NORMANDIE

COMTÉ DE
VERMANDOIS

DUCHÉ
DE
BRETAGNE

COMTÉ
D'ANJOU

DUCHÉ
DE
BOURGOGNE

DUCHÉ
D'AQUITAINE

DUCHÉ
DE
GASCOGNE

COMTÉ
DE
TOULOUSE

MARQUISAT
DE
GOTHIE

LOCATION OF
MONTREUIL-SUR-MER

2) What was the Revolt of the Earls?

In 1075, for reasons that are obscure, a powerful Breton earl named Ralph de Gaël devised a plan to rebel against – and perhaps even kill – William. Ralph seems to have come to England after 1066, and by 1069 he had succeeded his father as earl in East Anglia. As a substantial landholder in England he was a major beneficiary of the Conquest and defended Norwich against Danish attacks in 1069, so for a while was loyal to William's regime. In 1075, Ralph married Emma, the daughter of William fitz Osbern (d. 1071), who was one of the Conqueror's closest associates in the years immediately after Hastings. At the wedding feast, Ralph seems to have persuaded his new brother-in-law, Roger, Earl of Hereford, to participate in a rebellion against the king. Waltheof, Earl of Huntingdon, also allowed himself to be drawn into the conspiracy.

It is possible that all these men felt that their authority in their earldoms was more limited than that of their fathers, a result of William's policy of reducing the scope of what had been super-earldoms immediately after the Conquest. Certainly, Roger seems to have found intolerable the encroachment of royal sheriffs onto his lands. It is also true that the scale of their earldoms had been diminished: Ralph's authority seems to have been confined to East Anglia, whereas the earldom of his father had once embraced the whole of the east midlands; Roger felt that he should have inherited authority over the whole of western Wessex; and Waltheof's power was confined to the lands north of the Tees, whereas his father, Earl Siward, had held all Northumbria. It also seems likely that by revolting in 1075, the earls were taking advantage of William's absence from England at that time.

Source Investigation. Read Sources A–D and answer these questions:

a) Study Source A. What can you learn about the scale and character of the Revolt of the Earls from this source?

b) Study Sources B, C and D. Compare what these sources say about the attitude of Waltheof. How can you explain these differences?

> **Source A. *Anglo-Saxon Chronicle*. The *Chronicle* was first begun at the end of the ninth century. It is a contemporary record of events, written by monks in England.**
>
> [At the wedding celebrations of Earl Ralph] there was Earl Roger, and Earl Waltheof, and bishops, and abbots, who there agreed, that they would drive their royal lord [William] out of his kingdom. It was Earl Roger and Earl Ralph who were the authors of that plot; and who enticed the Bretons to them, and sent eastward to Denmark to try and obtain a fleet to assist them.

Source B. Florence of Worcester (1095–1140). The *Chronicle of Chronicles* was composed by a monk in Worcester in the first decades of the twelfth century.

Roger, earl of Hereford, son of William, earl of the same province, gave his daughter in marriage to Ralph, earl of East Anglia, against the command of the king; and while he was celebrating the marriage with much magnificence, along with a great multitude of nobles in the province of Cambridge, he formed a conspiracy [plot] in which most of the party joined against the king, and they compelled earl Waltheof, whom they had insidiously [through deliberate deception] surprised, to join the plot.

Source C. Orderic Vitalis, *The Ecclesiastical History*. Vitalis (1075–1142) wrote his *History* between 1123 and 1141. He was born in England to a Norman father and an English mother. From about the age of ten he entered the monastery in Normandy, where he remained for the rest of his life. (Orderic Vitalis here puts words into the mouths of the three earls.)

Ralph and Roger tell Waltheof: 'Join our party and stand with us; we can promise you a third of England. We wish to restore all the good customs that the realm of Albion [England] enjoyed in the time of the virtuous King Edward [the Confessor]. One of us shall be king and the other two dukes.' Waltheof replied: 'In such affairs the greatest caution is necessary; and every man in the country owes absolute loyalty to his liege lord. King William has lawfully received [from me] the oath of fealty which I his vassal rightly swore, and has given his niece to me in marriage as a pledge of lasting loyalty. He has given me a rich earldom and counted me amongst his closest friends. How can I be unfaithful to such a lord, unless I utterly desecrate [betray] my faith? I am known all over the country, and it would cause great scandal if – which Heaven forbid – I were publicly proclaimed a sacrilegious [Godless] traitor. The law of England punishes the traitor by beheading, and deprives his whole family of their just inheritance. Heaven forbid that I should stain my honour with the guilt of treachery, and that such shame should be voiced abroad [around the country] about me.' [Having declined the earls' invitation to join their plot, Waltheof is obliged to take 'a terrible oath' not to reveal their plans.]

Source D. William of Malmesbury. *Deeds of the Kings of the English*. William (d. c.1143) was a monk at Malmesbury Abbey in Wiltshire. He completed his *Deeds* in 1125. His father was a Norman and his mother English.

[Earl Ralph was] a man of whose nature was foreign to every good thing. He dreamed up a most unjust plot and when the guests had become intoxicated and heated with wine, he disclosed his intention in a long, aggressive speech. As their thinking was entirely clouded by drunkenness, they loudly applauded the orator. Here Roger, Earl of Hereford, brother to the wife of Ralph, and here Waltheof, together with many others, plotted to kill the king. [Waltheof, unable] to restrain his evil inclinations, could not preserve his loyalty [to the King].

3) How great was the threat posed by the Revolt of the Earls?

The threat posed by the Revolt of the Earls appears significant, not only because they were great landowners in England, but also because they sought help from their territories across the Channel. Ominously, the earls also invited participation from Denmark. In reality, the plan was overly ambitious and proved difficult to coordinate. Moreover, Waltheof seems to have had second thoughts and revealed all to Lanfranc, who then sent him to the king in Normandy. Roger and Ralph attempted to mobilize their earldoms, but the former was thwarted by Wulfstan, bishop of Worcester (who put himself at the head of a force that prevented Roger from crossing the river Severn), and the latter was unable to overcome Geoffrey, bishop of Countances, who forced Ralph to flee to Norwich from where he departed into exile, leaving his wife to hold for a while the castle against the royal army. Meanwhile, a great Danish fleet of some two hundred ships, having arrived only after the revolt had lost momentum, turned around and headed for home.

Question

1) Study Source A. What can you learn from this source about reasons for the failure of the Revolt of the Earls? Use your contextual knowledge to identify other reasons not mentioned in this source.

Source A. Florence of Worcester (1095–1140). The *Chronicle of Chronicles* was composed by a monk in Worcester in the first decades of the twelfth century.

> Wulfstan, bishop of Worcester, with a great force, Æthelwig, abbot of Evesham, with his followers, and having obtained the assistance of Urse, sheriff of Worcester, and Walter de Lacy, with their forces, and a large number of the people, prepared to prevent the earl of Hereford from crossing the Severn and joining earl Ralph and his army at the appointed place. Odo bishop of Bayeux, the king's brother, and Geoffrey, bishop of Coutances, with a great force, both of English and Normans, ready for action, met earl Ralph encamped near Cambridge.

4) What was the significance of the Revolt of the Earls of 1075?

Considering the dangerous potential of the revolt in 1075, perhaps its greatest significance lies in the fact that William felt sufficiently secure to leave its containment and defeat to his deputies. He stayed away from England until the point at which news broke of a possible Danish invasion. This, along with the fact that the rebels were overcome with a united force of English and Normans, provides strong evidence of the extent to which the Norman regime had established itself by 1075.

The Revolt of the Earls can also be seen as something of a turning point in the career of the Conqueror. After 1075 the task of keeping his conquests became more difficult, partly because of his age (he was approaching 50 in 1075) and his deteriorating relationships with those close to him, and partly because of the backlash to the revolt. William ordered that the rebels were harshly and cruelly treated: Earl Roger was deprived of his lands and suffered life imprisonment; many of the Bretons who had been involved on the orders of Earl Ralph were blinded and mutilated; and Earl Waltheof, who had immediately confessed the plot to Lanfranc, was sentenced to beheading – an unprecedented act since 1066.

The nature of Waltheof's fate led many to regard him as a martyr, even a saint. The cult that developed around his memory had a powerful anti-Norman flavour. Meanwhile, Ralph escaped back to Brittany, from where he continued his rebellion. From the castle of Dol – in Brittany but close to the Norman border – Ralph harassed William in Normandy. When William besieged Dol, Ralph gained the support of Philip I of France and together they defeated William – the first serious military check that he had suffered in France for more than twenty years. William never captured Ralph, who eventually died on the First Crusade in 1098 or 1099.

Question

1) Describe the short-term outcomes of the failure of the Revolt of the Earls.

---

5) Why did Robert Curthose (eldest son of William the Conqueror) revolt during 1078–80 and what were the consequences?

At the time he adopted a position of open revolt to his father, either in late 1077 or early 1078, Robert was around twenty-five years old. He had been designated as William's successor in Normandy when he was aged around twelve or thirteen, and had become increasingly impatient to wield influence and authority. From about 1068 it seems that Robert was made primarily responsible for the administration of the duchy, even on occasion using the title of duke and benefitting from his father's frequent absence from Normandy. However, in reality it is more likely that Matilda, Robert's mother, was responsible for the government of Normandy. Thus, already frustrated, Robert almost certainly became more so from 1072 when his father became almost permanently resident in Normandy.

Matters came to a head in an almighty family row at Laigle, Normandy, where Robert was visited by his younger brothers Henry and William. The last two seem to have provoked a brawl by urinating on Robert from the balcony of the hall. A reconciliation appears to have been effected by the arrival of their father, but the following night Robert withdrew from his father's court with a large group of followers. Indeed, chief among Robert's supporters were important men such as Robert de Bellême (son of Roger of Montgomery, Earl of Shrewsbury (d. 1094), probably the richest tenant-in-chief of William) and William de Breteuil (son of William fitz Osbern (d. 1071)). Robert's supporters could thus provide him with bases outside Normandy and the means with which to wage a war against his father. It was not long before William's enemies found in the rebel group a common point of focus. Thus, Robert's forces were joined by groups of men who had the backing of the duke of and the king of France. During the winter of 1078–79 Robert was making hit-and-run raids on Normandy from a castle at Gerberoi, given to him by the king of France.

William thus besieged Gerberoi for three weeks, eventually engaging the rebels in battle. Father and son engaged in single combat, during which Robert wounded William in the hand. The struggle was clearly bitter, and both sides were equally determined – William's horse was killed under him. William was driven off, though intermediaries eventually secured a reconciliation by 12 April 1080 in which Robert was confirmed as heir to Normandy.

The rivalry between William and Robert was also exploited by the Scottish king, Malcom III, who in 1079 launched a massive raid into northern

England that plundered the whole of the territory from the Tweed to the Tees. Ironically, following his reconciliation with his father, it was Robert, assisted by Odo, bishop of Bayeux, who forced back the Scots and brought Malcolm to the negotiating table.

Source Investigation: The rebellion of Robert Curthose

1) Study Sources A and B. Which source is more useful for a historian researching the quarrel between William and Robert Curthose? Explain your answer.

2) Study Sources C and D. Use your own knowledge to explain how accurate you consider these representations of events at Gerberoi. Explain your answer.

3) Study Source D. How convincing is this interpretation of the impact of the quarrel between William and Robert? Explain your answer using Interpretation A and your contextual knowledge.

> **Source A. Orderic Vitalis, *The Ecclesiastical History*. Vitalis wrote his *History* between 1123 and 1141. He was born in England to a Norman father and an English mother. From about the age of ten he entered the monastery in Normandy, where he remained for the rest of his life. Orderic here creates an imagined conversation between William and his son about the latter's entitlement to Normandy.**
>
> 'What you ask [to be given control of Normandy], my son, is not convenient. It was by Norman valour [strength] that I made the conquest of England. Normandy is mine by hereditary descent, and I will never, while I live, hand over the government.' Robert then said: 'but what am I to do, what have I to give to my followers?' His father answered: 'be obedient to me in all things, as becomes you, and be wisely content to share my power in all my dominions [territories] as a son under his father.' But Robert retorted: 'I desire to have an establishment of my own, that I may be able worthily to reward my supporters for their services. I therefore pray you give up to me the dukedom [of Normandy].' The King replied: 'what you ask, my son, is quite preposterous. It is shameful to wish to deprive your father of the dominions, which, if you are worthy, you will receive him in due course.' On hearing of his father's determination, Robert said: 'henceforth I shall serve strangers, and see whether by fortunes favour I cannot gain in exile those owners and advantages which are shamefully withheld from me in my father's house.' Having said this, Robert left his father's presence in great anger. [Father and son took up arms at Gerberoi where many men on either side] were unhorsed, horses were killed, and the combatants suffered considerably from the losses.

Source B. *Anglo-Saxon Chronicle*. The *Chronicle* was first begun at the end of the ninth century. It is a contemporary record of events, written by monks in England.

1079: in this year King William fought against his son, Robert, outside Normandy near a castle called Gerberoi. King William was wounded there, and the horse he rode was killed, and William, his [younger] son, was wounded there, and many men were killed.

Source C. The combat between William and Robert at Gerberoi 1079, as imagined by M. Mackinlay in c.1920.

Source D. The combat between William and Robert at Gerberoi 1079, as imagined by James William Edmund Doyle in 1864.

6) Who was Bishop Odo and why was he arrested in c.1082?

William's deteriorating relationships with a number of his closest associates is illustrated by the arrest in late in 1082 or early 1083 of Odo, the half-brother of William (they shared the same mother). In 1050, William had appointed Odo as bishop of Bayeux, and Odo had played a central role in the Conquest and the imposition of Norman rule in William's new kingdom. Yet following his arrest, Odo was put on trial in 1083, then imprisoned in Rouen in Normandy. He was released in 1087 upon the wish of the dying king.

Odo's importance to William earlier in his career was considerable. He supplied 100 ships for the invasion of 1066 and is shown prominently in the Bayeux Tapestry on at least two occasions – perhaps not surprising since he was the patron of this remarkable artefact. He was duly rewarded by William with grants of land in England. When William returned to Normandy in February 1067, Odo was appointed to act as joint regent with William fitz Osbern. He was also made Earl of Kent. In this role he played a key part in imposing Norman rule on that territory, including ensuring the loyalty of Dover when the castle there was attacked by Eustace of Boulogne (see p. 134).

Odo became one of the very greatest landholders in England. He seems to have acted consistently loyally and positively on behalf of William. Indeed, only Odo's seal (the device by which orders and grants were made) had the same status as that of the king's. Odo was present at most of the great ceremonies of state, such as Matilda's coronation in 1068 and William's crown-wearing ceremonies; he was fundamental to the quashing of the revolt of the three earls in 1075; he played a key role in resisting the Scottish invasion of 1080.

Odo's sudden arrest in either late 1082 or early 1083 is therefore something of a shock. What do the sources say about this event?

Source Investigation. Study Sources A–E.

a) Study Sources A, B and C. Using these sources and your own knowledge, describe the status and importance of Odo at the time of his arrest.

b) Study Sources D and E. What reasons do these Sources give for the arrest of Odo?

c) Study Source D. Explain what you think William meant by the remark 'I satisfied myself of this on several occasions and therefore I imprisoned, not the bishop, but the tyrannical earl.'

d) Use Sources A–C and your own knowledge to explain whether William was justified in his arrest of Odo.

e) Study Sources A–E. Using these sources, and your contextual knowledge, what do you think the arrest of Odo suggests about the security of the Norman regime by the 1080s? Explain your answer.

Source A. Scenes from the Bayeux Tapestry showing a) Odo (seated on the left) giving advice to William and b) fighting at the Battle of Hastings. (Odo is shown with a club in his hand because bishops were not supposed to wield weapons.) Odo commissioned the Bayeux Tapestry.

Source B. Seal of Odo. (A seal was wax moulded into an image and attached to documents to ensure their authenticity.) Taken after a lost original by P. de Farcy dans la 'Sigillographie de la Normandie', 1846.

THE SEAL OF ODO, BISHOP OF BAYEUX, HALF-BROTHER OF WILLIAM I.

Archæologia, vol. i.

Source C. Map showing the lands of Odo in England.

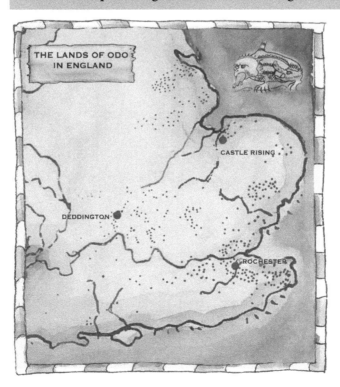

THE LANDS OF ODO IN ENGLAND

CASTLE RISING

DEDDINGTON

ROCHESTER

Source D. Orderic Vitalis, *The Ecclesiastical History*. Vitalis (1075–1142) wrote his *History* between 1123 and 1141. He was born in England to a Norman father and an English mother. From about the age of ten he entered the monastery in Normandy, where he remained for the rest of his life. This is Vitalis's version of William's deathbed speech.

'I have imprisoned for four years this Bishop [Odo], who, when he ought to have proved himself exemplary in the just government of England, became a most cruel oppressor of the people and the destroyer of monks. In desiring the liberation of this seditious [rebellious] man you are ill advised it is clear that my brother, Odo, is an untrustworthy man, ambitious, given to fleshly desires, and of enormous cruelty; and I am certain that he will never be converted from his womanising and ruinous follies. I satisfied myself of this on several occasions and therefore I imprisoned, not the bishop, but the tyrannical earl. There is no doubt that if he is released, he will disturb the whole country and be the ruin of thousands.'

Source E. William of Malmesbury. *Deeds of the Kings of the English*. William (d. c.1143) was a monk at Malmesbury Abbey in Wiltshire. He completed his *Deeds* in 1125. His father was a Norman and his mother English.

[Odo] had wonderful skill in accumulating treasure so that he had nearly purchased the Roman **papacy** [the office of pope] from the citizens. When there arose the rumour of his intended journey [to Rome to become pope after Gregory VII (r. 1073–85)], soldiers eagerly flocked to him from all parts of the kingdom. The king, alarmed, threw him into confinement, saying that he did not seize the bishop of Bayeux, but the earl of Kent. [Odo's] supporters, being intimidated by threats, revealed such quantities of gold that the heap of precious metal would surpass the belief of the present age; and many sackfuls of wrought gold were also taken out of the rivers, which Odo had secretly buried in certain places.

7) How significant was the renewed Scandinavian threat in 1085?

Cnut IV ascended the Danish throne in 1080 and quickly made it clear that he held the same ambitions towards the English throne as his predecessors. In other words, he sought to re-establish the great Anglo-Scandinavian kingdom presided over by this grandfather, Cnut (r. 1016–35). Having won the support of King Olaf III, king of Norway, Cnut set about preparing a great invasion fleet. News of these developments, as had happened in the past, led the other enemies of William to consider attacks upon England. Thus, William's son, Robert Curthose (whose sister was married to Cnut IV) once again took to the field with the active support of Philip of France. Meanwhile King Malcolm stood poised on the Scottish border.

The threat posed was sufficiently significant for William to leave Normandy. Once in England he immediately caused certain of the coastal districts of England to be laid waste in order to deny provisions to any invading force. According to the *Anglo-Saxon Chronicle*, he also brought with him 'a larger force of mounted men and foot soldiers than had ever come into this country'. The invasion, however, never materialized: Cnut IV, never popular amongst his own subjects, was murdered in 1086.

Question

1) Assess the scale of the threat that faced William in 1085. Explain your answer.

8) Why was there a rebellion of leading magnates in 1088?

William the Conqueror's death in 1087 precipitated a period of turmoil, advanced by his deathbed decision to divide Normandy and England between his two eldest sons, Robert and William Rufus. His decision immediately created a dilemma for the leading magnates: which of the two sons should they follow?

In order to resolve this dilemma the leading magnates resolved upon forming a league to depose or kill William Rufus. Six of the greatest landholders recorded in Domesday, headed by the recently released Odo, joined the rebellion against William Rufus. From the spring of 1088 they devastated the lands of men loyal to Robert and garrisoned their castles. However, their rebellion failed in the face of the military determination of William and the ongoing absence (in Normandy) of Robert. Odo was captured and went into exile in Normandy, dying in 1097 on the First Crusade. Nevertheless, magnates with lands on both sides of the Channel could not easily serve both king and duke when those leaders were hostile towards each other. Thus, instability and conflicts continued until the Conqueror's third son, Henry I (the successor in England to William Rufus in 1100), defeated his brother Duke Robert at the Battle of Tinchebrai in 1106 and henceforth ruled, like his father, as both duke and king.

Questions

1) Study Source A. Put the argument presented in this source into your own words.

2) Study Source B. How far do you agree with this interpretation? Explain your answer.

Source A. Orderic Vitalis, *The Ecclesiastical History*. Vitalis (1075–1142) wrote his *History* between 1123 and 1141. He was born in England to a Norman father and an English mother. From about the age of ten he entered the monastery in Normandy, where he remained for the rest of his life. Here he has imagined a conversation among Norman nobles after the death of William I.

'What are we to do? Now that William [the Conqueror] is dead, two young men have succeeded and eagerly divided the lordship of England and Normandy. How can we properly serve two lords who are so different and so distant from each other? If we serve Robert, Duke of Normandy, worthily, we will offend his brother, William, and we will be stripped by him of our great revenues and large estates in England. On the other hand, if we obey King William fittingly, Duke Robert will deprive us of all our inherited lands in Normandy.'

Source B. David Bates, *William the Conqueror* (1964).

The collapse [in governance from 1088] must be seen as a commentary on the Conqueror's achievements. It is quite wrong to blame the turmoil exclusively on the ambitions of his sons or on the turbulence of the aristocracy; it was William after all who had divided up his lands in the first place and had pressed his authority harshly onto the Normans. The disturbed scene proves, if nothing else does, how William's policies and attitudes had been geared to his own lifetime, and not beyond. Yet in the midst of this chaotic situation, we can see what William's true achievements were. His great achievement, and the true basis of his greatness, was to give Norman rule in England and the union of Normandy and England such stability that his successors should want both to continue.

Questions

1) Look back over pages 173–175. For each of the rebellions from 1085 to 1088 create a graphical representation of the scale of the threat posed by each. (Use the same criteria as those you used in Question 1 on page 138).

2) Look back over Chapter 5. Were the rebellions 1075–88 more or less of a threat to the Crown's authority than the rebellions of 1067–71? Explain your answer.

3) To what extent was the Norman regime in England destabilized by rebellions and threats of invasion from 1075 to 1088? You may refer to the following in your answer:

   • threats from Scandinavia

   • actions of Robert Curthose

   • activities of Odo

---

9) Exam practice and online resources

Questions in the style of Edexcel

a) 4 marks

i) Describe two key features of the Revolt of the Earls.

b) 12 marks per question

i) Explain why leading earls revolted in 1075. You may use the following in your answer:

   • Philip, King of France

   • Ralph de Gael

You must also use information of your own.

ii) Explain why Robert Curthose participated in rebellion against his father, William, in 1078. You may use the following in your answer:

   • Normandy

   • succession

You must also use information of your own.

iii) Explain why there was a disputed succession to the English throne when William I died. You may use the following in your answer:

   • Normandy

   • Bishop Odo

You must also use information of your own.

c) 16 marks per question

i) 'The most significant threat that William faced after 1071/72 was the rebellion of Robert Curthose. How far do you agree? You may use the following in your answer:

- Odo
- Cnut IV

You must also use information of your own.
    (Refer back to Chapter 5 to help you answer this question.)

ii) 'The greater threats to William's authority occurred in the years up to 1071–1072; after that time his regime was increasingly secure'. How far do you agree? You may use the following in your answer:

- Danish invasion of 1069
- Robert Curthose

You must also use information of your own.

Questions in the style of AQA

a) 8 marks per question

i) Study Source A. How convincing is this interpretation of Robert's relationship with his father, William? Explain your answer using Interpretation A and your contextual knowledge.

Source A. Robert Curthose asking his father's pardon after their clash at Gerberoi.

ii) Study Source B. How convincing is this interpretation of the effects of the quarrel between William I and his eldest son, Robert? Explain your answer using Interpretation A and your contextual knowledge.

Source B. David Bates, *William the Conqueror* (2004).

The effects of this quarrel [between father and son] were profoundly damaging to William and to his power. A family which had previously carried all before it was now divided. Matilda was torn between loyalty and affection for husband and son. The king was detained permanently in Normandy and could not cross to England when he wished to do so. The Norman aristocracy was divided by the quarrel, since members of the younger generation of a number of families supported Robert. This was civil war at its bitterest and most desolating which also gave William's northern French enemies a chance to attack him.

b) 8 marks per question

Explain why the Revolt of the Earls has been seen as a turning point in the history of William's rule in England.

i) Explain why Odo was arrested in c.1082.

ii) Explain why leading magnates rebelled in 1085.

c) 8 marks per question

i) Write an account of the causes and consequences of the Revolt of the Earls.

ii) Write an account of the renewed Scandinavian threat of 1085.

Online Resources

Lucy Martin from UEA examines the detail of the 1075 rebellion and explains why it is significant in the history of the Norman Conquest of England https://www.uea.ac.uk/history/podcasts.

Short biography of Odo http://news.bbc.co.uk/local/kent/hi/people_and_places/history/newsid_8720000/8720806.stm.

Detailed timeline of the rebellions faced by William, 1067–80 http://www.englandsnortheast.co.uk/NorthConquered.html.

7 THE NORMAN CHURCH AND MONASTICISM, 1066–1100

Key Issues

Timeline

1070: Most Anglo-Saxon bishops are replaced by Normans; Stigand is replaced by Lanfranc as archbishop of Canterbury

1072: Canterbury achieves primatial (first-order) status over York

1075: Lanfranc presides over the first of a number of reforming councils

1073: Gregory VII elected pope

1075: *Dictatus Papae* – a document produced by the papacy claiming that the pope had supreme authority over kings and all churchmen; it marked the beginning of the Investiture Controversy

1085: Death of Gregory VII

1089: Death of Lanfranc; archiepiscopal see of Canterbury left vacant by William II

1093: Anselm nominated archbishop of Canterbury

Overview

Long before 1066 England had become a Christian country and those who lived within its boundaries worshipped according to rites and beliefs devised and spread by the head of the church, the pope in Rome. (This form of Christianity is thus known as Roman Catholicism.) The church had a threefold presence throughout England: physical, in the form of its cathedrals, monasteries and parish churches (most villages had a church by this time, increasingly built from stone); spiritual, in that it provided religious services throughout the country and offered the opportunity for penance (an act designed to atone for a sin); and political, in that its leading churchmen had enormous power and authority as a result of their literacy, their administrative capacity, and, above all, the land they possessed.

1) What do we mean by 'the church' in England on the eve of the Conquest?

i) The organization of the church

The 'church' refers to an organization, hierarchical in nature, staffed by individuals with titles such as 'bishop' at the upper level and 'priest' at the lower level. These men, for there were no women priests or bishops, were responsible for providing spiritual support and religious services (such as baptism, marriages and burials) for all aristocrats, townsfolk and peasants. There were also religious communities of men (monks) and women (nuns), who lived typically under vows of poverty and a strict adherence to rules that focused on the worship of God. These communities of monks and nuns lived in specially constructed buildings, known as monasteries and nunneries respectively. (See pages 188–189.)

The men of the church, the 'clergy', i.e. priests and bishops, composed a significant minority of the population. Indeed, by the thirteenth century about every one man in fifty was a churchman. The highest church office in England was 'archbishop'. There were two archbishops, one based at York and the other at Canterbury. An archbishop had authority over a bishop. Archbishops and bishops (known collectively as the **episcopate**) were each responsible for administering a specific territory known as a diocese (or a 'see'). England had 16 dioceses by 1066.

Dioceses were divided into smaller units for administrative convenience, the smallest of which was the parish. This was broadly equivalent to a village, or a vill, and, indeed, many vills and parishes were overlapping units with the same name. There were around nine thousand medieval parishes in England of varying size. Each parish had its own church, a building in which worship took place for all residents of the parish: every person was expected to attend their parish church, and a refusal to do so was regarded as heresy, a most serious offence. Within each diocese was a principal church housing the bishop's *cathedra*, a Latin word meaning 'seat' or 'throne'. These important churches are thus called cathedrals, and were built on a much greater scale than parish churches to reflect the prestige of the bishop, the occasional need to accommodate very large congregations of people, and to house the remains of important saints. For example, the enormous and imposing cathedral of Durham was the seat of the bishop of Durham, who played an important additional military role in the region to defend England against the Scots and whose cathedral housed the remains of Saint Cuthbert (d. 687). These buildings thus became important centres of pilgrimage (places where people would travel to pray to a particular saint) and grew rich as a consequence.

Alongside its distinct organization, the church also had its own courts and legal procedures informed by a body of law known as canon law. Any member of the church accused of a crime could argue that he or she should be tried in a church court, a privilege which caused increasing tension with the king, who believed that the royal courts had greater status than those of the church.

Questions

1) Explain what you understand by the following terms:
   - archbishop
   - bishop
   - episcopate
   - diocese/see
   - pope
   - clergy
   - Roman Catholicism
   - canon law

2) Study Source A.
   a) What can you learn from this source about the religious condition of England before 1066?
   b) How reliable do you consider this source? Use the details of the source and your own knowledge to explain your answer.

Source A. William of Malmesbury, *History of Recent Events*, written 1140–42. William's father was Norman, and his mother was English. He spent his adult life as a monk in Malmesbury Abbey in England.

> The love of learning and of religion [had] decayed for some years before the coming of the Normans. The clergy, contented with a very slight measure of learning, could scarcely stammer out the words of the sacraments, and a person who understood grammar was an object of wonder and astonishment. The monks mocked the rule of their order with fine vestments and with the use of every kind of food. The nobility, given up to luxury and wantonness [excessive leisure] did not go to church in the early morning after the manner of Christians, but merely in a casual manner heard matins and mass [important church services] from a hurrying priest in their chambers amid the blandishments [flattering remarks] of their wives. [However] after their coming to England [the Normans] revived the rule of religion which had there grown lifeless. You might see churches rise in every village, and, in the towns and the cities, [new] monasteries [were built]. You could watch the country flourishing with renewed religious observance.

ii) The political importance of the church

When William came to the throne in 1066, according to Domesday Book, the church controlled between a third and a quarter of the landed wealth of England, which had been acquired in part by people gifting their land to the church in the hope that this would ease their passage to heaven. In return for this land, William demanded knight's service from his bishops because they were major landlords holding land directly from the king as tenants-in-chief, just like the earls.

As we saw on page 33, the episcopate played an essential part in the government of the kingdom: bishops were often recruited to serve as advisers to the king, as royal justices sitting in the shire courts and as generals in the royal armies. In an age when the king had no civil service, no police force and no regular army, the bishops were very significant agents of the Crown. It was, therefore, of immense importance to the king that he preserve the right to make appointments to episcopal positions. It was thus not through military might alone that the Normans imposed their will.

Question

1) Explain why it was important for the king to be able to appoint men of his choice as bishops.

iii) The physical presence of the church

The ways in which the Normans built or rebuilt churches – on a grander scale, in stone and with a distinct physical presence – were as significant as the ways in which they built their castles: they helped establish the presence and aura of the new regime. No major English church survived the first 50 years of Norman rule unchanged, with the single exception of Westminster Abbey. By 1087 no fewer than nine of England's fifteen Anglo-Saxon cathedrals had been burned down or demolished. This process was aided by Archbishop Lanfranc's decision to reorganize a number of the existing Anglo-Saxon bishoprics, resulting in the abandonment and decay of the associated church and the construction of a new Norman cathedral from scratch in the new location (see p. 192).

New Norman churches were built in a style that has become known as **Romanesque**, which imitated the architecture of ancient Rome, using semi-circular arches decorated with pointed, pyramid-shaped carvings called 'dog-tooth', sometimes accompanied with other rhythmic, patterned carvings. Durham Cathedral was built in this new style almost throughout, and on an immense scale. To the indigenous population – not yet recovered from the 'harrying' of the north (see Chapter 5) – it must have seemed awe inspiring and intimidating. This rebuilding was even evident at the local level of parish churches, although not on the same scale as cathedrals. Anglo-Saxon parish churches were added to and developed by the Normans, thus juxtaposing the Norman style of semicircular arches with the earlier Anglo-Saxon style of much smaller, slit-like windows.

Questions

1) Study Source A. What can you learn from this source about episcopal sees in England in 1066?

2) Study Source B. Identify two features of this doorway that reveal it to be Norman.

3) Study Sources C and D. Use the details in these sources and your own knowledge to explain why Durham Cathedral was built on such a scale and in Romanesque style.

4) Study Source E. Explain why the replacement of Anglo-Saxon cathedrals by the Normans was so extensive.

Source A. The dioceses in England in 1066.

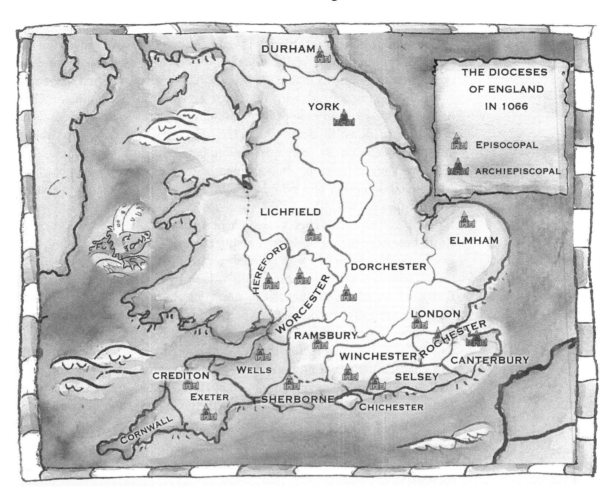

Source B. Main entrance to Selby Abbey. Built in the eleventh century.

Source C. Durham Cathedral, in the north of England.

Source D. A view of the interior of Durham Cathedral. Built in the eleventh century.

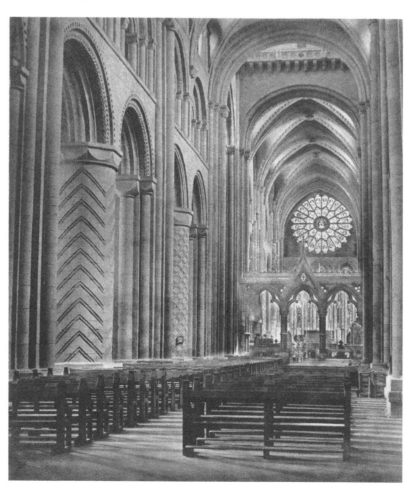

Source E. Marc Morris, *The Norman Conquest* (2013).

[The great rebuilding of important churches by the Normans] was a revolution. The single greatest in the history of the English ecclesiastical [religious] architecture. Visit any of these churches today, and you will not find a single piece of standing pre-Conquest masonry. So total was the Norman renaissance [rebirth] that no cathedral was entirely rebuilt in England until the early thirteenth century, when Salisbury was moved from Sarum.

2) What do we mean by the term 'monasticism'?

A monastery was a set of purpose-built buildings designed to accommodate a religious community. Each community belonged to a particular 'order' and lived according to that order's 'rule', which was a strict set of instructions for daily routine, religious services and conduct. This form of living is known as monasticism. In the late eleventh century all Western monasteries belonged to the Benedictine order, which lived according to the rule written by St Benedict in the sixth century (see Source B, p. 190), or to the Cluniac order, which was a slight variant on the Benedictine rule. In the twelfth century other orders were founded, such as the Cistercians and the Augustinians, which made more severe amendments to the basic rule of St Benedict.

Monasteries were first established in the British Isles in the sixth and seventh centuries, although many of those in England and Scotland were subsequently destroyed by pagan Scandinavian settlers. There had been a revival of monasticism by the time of the Norman Conquest, when there were around fifty monasteries for men and ten nunneries in England. The Norman aristocracy were avid founders of monasteries, with a particular regard for the Cluniac order, and by the end of the eleventh century they had added to this number.

New foundations established in the immediate wake of the Conquest included abbeys at Selby (1068), Shrewsbury (c.1085), Chester (1093) and Colchester (1095). William established a new foundation on Senlac Hill, the site of the Battle of Hastings, known thereafter as Battle Abbey. He insisted that the altar stone should occupy the very spot where Harold was killed. A unique feature of the English monastic arrangement was the existence of 'monastic cathedrals', in which the church doubled as both the cathedral for a diocese and the monastic church of a community of Benedictine monks, as at Canterbury, Ely, Norwich and Worcester.

Monks wore a distinctive outer garment, called a habit, and had the top of their head shaved, producing a style called a 'tonsure'. The daily life of monks revolved around a routine of prayer and religious services (often six each day) in the monastic church, scholarship (reading and writing) in the abbey buildings and work on its land. The monks would include in their services prayers for the souls of their patron and other benefactors (i.e. those who had given money), which meant that many monasteries grew rich through bequests of property, donated in the return for prayers being said for the souls of benefactors. Monks were trained to read and write, and to manage their estates, which meant that monasteries were also therefore effective management schools, and heads of monasteries were sometimes promoted to become bishops. Monasteries were also economic powerhouses. They were important centres of consumption, stimulating trade and demand for luxury goods, and significant local employers. They developed their properties, investing in mills, controlling fairs and building bridges and causeways over rivers. Their estates produced crops, livestock, wool, stone, tin, lead and silver, and their households brewed ale and baked bread in vast quantities. As landlords they also wielded authority over townsfolk and many rural peasants. The head of a monastery – the 'abbot' or, if a nunnery, the 'abbess' – thus carried significant local and regional influence, and could be appointed by the king to undertake other duties on his behalf. Hence the king insisted on appointing the leading abbots and abbesses for the same reason that he claimed the authority to appoint to bishops.

Question

1) Study Sources A, B and C. Use Sources A–C and your own knowledge to explain what you understand by the term 'monasticism'.

Source A. St Benedict delivering his Rule to St. Maurus and other monks of his order France, Monastery of St. Gilles, Nimes, 1129.

Source B. Extracts from the Rule of St Benedict. (There are 73 chapters in total.)

Chapters 39 and 40 regulate the quantity and quality of the food. Two meals a day are allowed, with two cooked dishes at each. Each monk is allowed a pound of bread and a hemina (probably about half a pint) of wine. The flesh of four-footed animals is prohibited except for the sick and the weak.

Chapter 41 prescribes the hours of the meals, which vary with the time of year.

Chapter 42 enjoins the reading an edifying book in the evening, and orders strict silence after Compline [the evening church service]

Chapters 43–46 define penalties for minor faults, such as coming late to prayer or meals.

Chapter 47 requires the abbot to call the brothers to the 'work of God' (Opus Dei) [prayer and worship] in choir, and to appoint chanters [singers of divine office] and readers [those who would read from the Bible to their brethren].

Chapter 48 emphasizes the importance of daily manual labour appropriate to the ability of the monk. The hours of labour vary with the season but are never less than five hours a day.

Source C. A plan of Durham Cathedral showing the monastic buildings.

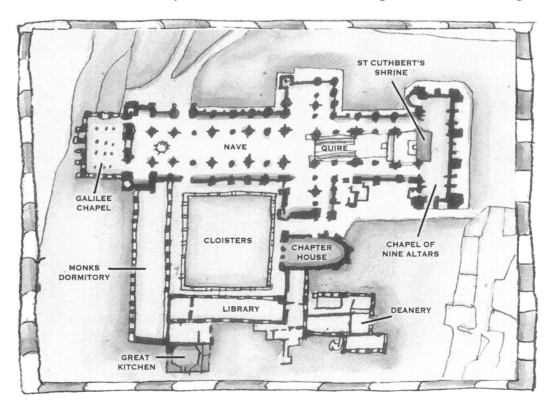

3) What was the 'Normanization' of the church and when did it occur?

The 'Normanization' of the church is the term used to describe the processes by which William increased his influence over the English church and brought it into line with practices of that in Normandy. At a basic level, this involved the replacement of existing abbots and bishops with men loyal to the Anglo-Norman regime, but it also involved reforms to the administration of the church, the promotion of new forms of monasticism and, as we have seen, the rebuilding of churches in a grand architectural style.

Since leading churchmen were so powerful, and could thus help or hinder the delivery of royal governance, William deposed a considerable number of bishops and abbots in office in 1066 and replaced them (mostly) with Normans. William needed bishops whom he could trust absolutely and who could act as his deputies. After 1070, only three English-born bishops remained in place. William also ousted many Anglo-Saxon abbots: 13 of the 21 abbots who attended the archbishop of Canterbury's council in 1075 were Anglo-Saxons, but by 1086 only 3 Anglo-Saxon abbots remained. Of all of these deposed churchmen, the highest-profile casualty was Stigand, archbishop of Canterbury, who in 1070 was replaced by Lanfranc, a 60-year-old Italian abbot who had been resident in Normandy.

Stigand had been appointed archbishop of Canterbury in 1052 by Edward the Confessor in 1052, replacing the Norman Robert of Jumieges (r. 1051–52), who had fallen from favour after the return of the Godwins (see p. 88). William could claim strong grounds for removing Stigand, because Stigand was not only the archbishopric of Canterbury but also the bishop of Winchester, and holding two major offices at once was against canon law. Several popes had excommunicated Stigand (the church's equivalent of outlawry, through which a person was officially excluded from the services of the Christian Church and thus denied access to Heaven at their death) in order to compel him to give up one of his sees, but Stigand had resisted. William therefore enjoyed papal support for the deposition of Stigand in 1070, who remained imprisoned until his death in 1072.

Question

1) What do you understand by the 'Normanization' of the church? Explain your answer.

4) How did Lanfranc help establish Norman authority?

The appointment of Lanfranc as archbishop of Canterbury in 1070 strengthened William's control of the English Crown by strengthening his control over the English church, which in turn enabled him to undertake a range of reforms of the Anglo-Saxon church.

i) Lanfranc established the primacy (i.e. the higher authority) of Canterbury over York

The archbishops of Canterbury and York had long been in dispute, because the former claimed authority over the latter, whereas the archbishop of York claimed independent overview of all of the northern dioceses. The dispute was rekindled in 1069 following the death of Ealdred (archbishop of York at the time of the Conquest). Lanfranc demanded that Ealdred's replacement, the Norman Thomas of Bayeux, should formally promise loyalty to him (an act known as a 'profession of obedience'), which in effect meant that the new archbishop of York accepted that the office of the archbishop of Canterbury was superior. Thomas asked the pope to intervene.

By 1072, Lanfranc had persuaded the papacy (i.e. the office or authority of the pope) that, as archbishop of Canterbury, he should have primatial (i.e. superior) status over all English dioceses. In establishing that the archbishop of Canterbury was the most senior churchman in England, Lanfranc reduced the power of future archbishops of York, which also diminished their usefulness as allies to any future rebels. Thereafter the archbishop of Canterbury had the undisputed authority to crown the kings of England, so that royal control over this office – which William enjoyed after 1070 – increased the security of the king.

ii) Lanfranc encouraged monasticism

Lanfranc was determined to ensure that monks should adhere rigorously to the rules of their order, and that monasticism should be encouraged and advanced. In 1066, only three of the fifteen English bishoprics were served by monastic chapters (Canterbury, Winchester and Worcester). Fifty years later there were a further seven monastic cathedrals established: Durham, Bath, Chester, Coventry, Norwich, Rochester and Ely. In total, around 34 new monasteries had been founded during the period 1066–87. The number of monks also rose: between 1066 and 1135 the number of monks and nuns increased from about one thousand to nearly five thousand. Between 1072 and 1104 the number of monks at Gloucester abbey rose from 10 to 100.

Under Lanfranc's guidance, a new monastic order – the Cluniacs, an off-shoot of the Benedictines – was established in England. The Cluniacs were a highly centralized order, the abbot of Cluny in France being the superior (head) of all its houses. It had 24 English houses by 1135. The creation of a new monastery required a sizeable endowment of land in order to provide sufficient income to support it, and only noble men and women possessed sufficient reserves of land to found monasteries: the grant of the land was in return for prayers to be said by the monks for the benefactors in perpetuity. The most significant of the new Cluniac foundations was that at Lewes in Sussex (dedicated to St Pancras), established after 1078 by William de Warenne, a Norman nobleman who became Earl of Surrey, and his wife Gunrada, a Flemish noblewoman.

Question

1) Study Source A. What can you learn from this source about how and why religious houses were founded?

Source A. Charter of William de Warenne in which he and his wife found the priory of Lewes, 1078.

> Be it known to all the faithful that I, William de Warrene, and my wife, Gundrada, for the redemption [saving] of our souls, and with the advice and assent of our lord, William, king of the English, give to God and to the holy apostles Peter and Paul at a place called Cluny, where the lord Abbot presides, the church of St Pancras in the same land of the English with all the things which pertain [relate] to it. I king William for the sake and safety of my kingdom and the salvation of my soul, and at the fervent request and petition of William de Warenne and Gundrada, his wife, confirm with our seal the gift recorded which they make to the holy apostles of God at the place called Cluny.

iii) Lanfranc held a series of reforming councils

Lanfranc held a series of councils to discuss and implement reforms to the church. After the councils of Winchester and Windsor in 1072, when the issue of the primacy was settled, Lanfranc held councils at London (1075, 1078), Winchester (1076) and Gloucester (1080, 1085). These councils issued church laws (canons) dealing with a number of issues. Amongst other things, the canons ensured that the profile and influence of the bishops was enhanced by ordering the relocation of three bishoprics from villages to major centres: Dorchester-on-Thames moved to Lincoln (1072); Selsey moved to Chichester (1075); and Sherborne moved to Salisbury. Other reforms stipulated that instances of clerical corruption and immorality be no longer tolerated. The practice of simony (buying and selling of church offices) was banned; that of celibacy (abstaining from sexual relations) was promoted with new vigour; and that of reading spiritual works was given renewed emphasis. Practices considered superstitious were banned. For example, bones or dead animals should not be hung up anywhere to avoid disease.

Question

1) Study Source A. What can you learn from this source about the authority of Lanfranc?

Source A. Letter of Lanfranc to the bishop of Thetford (undated).

> Give up the dice [gambling], to mention nothing worse, and the worldly amusements in which you are said to spend the whole day. Read sacred authors, and devote particular study to the decrees [rules] of the Roman pontiffs [popes] and to the sacred canons. Then you will find out what you do not know; having read them, you will deem worthless the devices in which you trust to evade Church discipline.

iv) Lanfranc bolstered support for the Crown

Lanfranc accepted and promoted the custom that the church councils were subject to the ultimate authority of the king, and he also ensured that the church acted in various ways which bolstered royal authority. For instance, he ordered that the clergy should express loyalty to the king publicly, thereby buttressing the Norman regime. More dramatically, when Odo (bishop of Bayeux and Earl of Kent) and William of St-Calais (bishop of Durham from 1080) were apprehended for plotting against the king in 1082 and 1088 respectively, Lanfranc argued that, as leading landholders in their own right (alongside the lands they controlled as bishops), each should be tried in the king's court rather than the church courts. This resulted in a harsher judgement than would have been served in the church courts and underlined the authority of the king. (Odo was imprisoned until 1087; St-Calais fled to Normandy.) Lanfranc also fulfilled the deathbed wishes of William I by crowning as king his second son, William – subsequently known as William Rufus – even though there was significant opinion amongst many of the tenants-in-chief that Robert Curthose (William I's eldest son) should inherit all of the cross-Channel territories.

All of this does not necessarily mean that Lanfranc subordinated the church to the Crown. Rather, his actions and policies suggest that he recognized that each institution grew stronger by working together. It was thus a symbiotic relationship (i.e. mutually beneficial). This can be seen in the occasions when Lanfranc acted as a leading official of royal government: he acted as regent on occasions when William was absent in Normandy; and he played a key part in detecting and defusing the revolt of the earls in 1075 (see p. 162).

Source Investigation. Study Sources A–C

1) Study Sources A and B. What do Sources A and B suggest about the relationship between William and Lanfranc? Explain your answer.

2) Study Source B. What can you learn from this source about why relations between the Crown and the church were sometimes strained?

3) Study Source C. How far do you agree with the interpretation put forward by Bates in Source C? Explain your answer using your contextual knowledge.

4) Refer to sections i)–iv) above. Assess the contribution made by Lanfranc to the consolidation of Norman rule.

Source A. Writ of William I, April 1072.

Be it known that if anyone, puffed up with pride, shall refuse to come to the bishop's court [to resolve matters related to the 'rule of the souls', such as adultery, and disputes over wills and burials], he shall be summoned three times, and if, after this, he shall still fail to appear, he shall be excommunicated; and if the strength and justice of the king and his sheriff shall be needed to carry this into effect, this support will be forthcoming. Anyone failing to appear at the bishop's court after one summons shall pay the appropriate penalty according to episcopal law. By virtue of my authority I also forbid any sheriff or reeve or officer of the king or any layman to interfere with the laws which relate to the bishop.

Source B. Extract from the trial of William of St-Calais, bishop of Durham, in the court of King William II (also known as William Rufus). The author of this account is unknown, but it was clearly written by someone connected with the church of Durham, who was apparently an eyewitness to the events he describes.

Then Lanfranc said to the King: 'if the bishop [St-Calais] continues to refuse you his castle, you may just justly take him into custody. He seeks to show that your barons are breaking faith with him, but in fact it is he who has broken faith.' Then Ralph Peverel and all the laymen present started to shout together: 'Seize him! [St-Calais] Seize him! Well he [Lanfranc] has spoken, this trusty old liegeman.' [Then Lanfranc continued,] 'Throw yourself without delay on [the king's] mercy and do not further question the judgement of this court.' 'God forbid', declared the bishop, 'that I should accept any judgement or one that violates the law of the Church.'

Source C. From D. Bates, *William the Conqueror* (1964).

William's support for the Church in England was reciprocated [returned] as the new Norman bishops and abbots lent their weight to the enforcement of the Norman Conquest. The mutual self-interest of king and Church is especially well illustrated by the requirements of the Church meeting held at Winchester at Easter 1072 that every priest in England say three masses [important prayers] for the king's health, and that anyone who spoke treason against William or his rule should be excommunicated. If the Norman soldiers did not catch the English rebels, then the clergy would!

5) What was the Investiture Controversy?

Gregory VII (r. 1073–85) was one of the great reforming popes, who had the ambition and determination to increase the rights and responsibilities of the papacy, with the aim that the pope would be the supreme authority in Europe. This ambition would inevitably test the power of the pope against the power of kings. In 1075, he issued a set of rulings called the *Dictatus Papae*, which set out the rights of the papacy, including, for example, that only the pope (i.e. not kings) had the right to depose bishops, and to move them from one see to another; the pope had the right to depose kings and to absolve subjects of their oath of fealty to kings who ruled badly; and anybody could appeal to the pope for justice, and kings were not to stop them.

Some rulers objected to Gregory's policy, on the basis that it threatened their power. For this reason Gregory was locked in conflict with Henry IV, Holy Roman Emperor (r. 1084–1105). Their dispute came to be known as the 'Investiture Controversy', because the emperor objected to the pope's decree that rulers were not allowed to control the appointment of bishops (i.e. to 'invest' them with their symbols of office). Pope Gregory wanted to ensure that bishops were not under the sway of kings, and that only the most qualified and dedicated candidates were appointed to jobs that entailed responsibility for the souls of the Christian people. The emperor, however, felt that he was entitled to appoint bishops, because they were important landholders with responsibilities to king and kingdom. Eventually, the emperor was forced to back down, and submit to the pope in a dramatic ceremony at Canossa (in Italy).

The term 'Investiture Controversy' thus refers specifically to the dispute between Pope Gregory VII and the Emperor Henry IV, but it also stands for the broader dispute between the pope and other monarchs about the extent of the pope's powers over kings and kingdoms.

Question

1) Study Source A. Using Source A and your own knowledge, explain what you understand by the term 'Investiture Crisis'.

Source A. A modern representation of a medieval monarch 'investing' a bishop.

6) Why did King William feel threatened by Pope Gregory VII's rulings?

Gregory made three particular demands upon William and Lanfranc: that English bishops must make regular visits to Rome to attend papal councils; that William must resume a payment to the papacy known as Peter's Pence (a regular payment to the papacy made by Anglo-Saxon kings); and, most provocatively, that William take an oath of fealty to Gregory, that is, that the king accept the pope as his feudal lord. Gregory believed that since William had sought the papacy's permission to invade England in 1066, and since the invasion had been successful, he owed his kingdom to the pope.

From William's point of view, it would not be right for a king to concede these demands because to do so would mean that he, and his successors, would lose ultimate control of their government. However, William was able to avoid meeting these demands without suffering the penalty of **excommunication** (which had been inflicted upon Emperor Henry IV), which would have undermined William's power. His ability to evade the difficult was probably due in part to the diplomacy of Lanfranc.

Questions

1) Study Source A. What reasons does Gregory suggest for Lanfranc's failure to visit the papacy? Which of these reasons do you find most credible? Explain your answer.

2) Study Sources B and C. What reasons does William provide in Source C for refusing to give 'full obedience' referred to in Source B? How compelling do you find his reasons? Explain your answer.

3) Study Source D. If William had indeed proved himself 'more worthy of approval and honour than other kings', why was Pope Gregory so keen for him to submit? Use this Source and your own knowledge to explain your answer.

Source A. Letter from Pope Gregory VII to Archbishop Lanfranc, 25 March 1079.

> We [Pope Gregory] have learned from a reliable source that your presence has been denied to us either through fear of the king – whom indeed we have always peculiarly cherished above others of that rank – or mainly through your own fault. [If you had been mindful of our support of you] neither fear of the secular power nor inordinate regard for any other person would have withheld you from our presence. So, then, [it falls to you] to correct your excess of negligence and to hasten as often as possible to present yourself before us in accordance with our wishes and often repeated commands.

Source B. Letter from Pope Gregory VII to William I, 24 April 1080.

> The higher you climb in rank and power the better disposed you are to show [thanks to God]. Now, therefore, I give you, as to a very dear son and one faithful to Saint Peter and ourself [Gregory], and in a few words, my advice as to how you should conduct yourself in future. I advise you strongly in true and not counterfeit charity, and for your own honour and safety, to give full obedience.

Source C. Letter from William I to Pope Gregory VII (c.1080).

> Your legate [representative] has insisted that I profess allegiance to you and your successors, and to think better regarding the money [Peter's Pence] which my predecessors were in the habit of sending to the Church of Rome. I have consented to the one but not to the other. I have not consented to pay fealty, nor will I now [do so] because I never promised it, nor do I find that my predecessors ever paid fealty to your predecessors.

Source D. Letter from Pope Gregory VII to Hugh bishop of Die, and Amatus, bishop of Oleron.

> The king of the English, although in certain matters he does not comport [behave] himself as devoutly as we might hope, nevertheless has in all the following respects shown himself more worthy of approval and honour than other kings: he has neither destroyed nor sold the churches of God; he has taken care to govern his subjects in peace and justice; he has refused his assent to anything detrimental to the apostolic see [the papacy]; and he has compelled the priests on oath to put away [renounce] their wives.

7) What was the nature of the relationship between William II (r. 1087–1100) and the church?

Lanfranc died in 1089, two years after William II had become king. The new monarch decided to leave the office of archbishop of Canterbury vacant, in order to take the substantial revenues of the Canterbury lands for himself. However, suffering a serious illness in 1093, he believed himself to be dying: he therefore decided to fill the vacancy, so that he could meet God with a clear conscience.

William II's choice of successor to Lanfranc was Anselm, Abbot of Bec. There immediately arose significant tensions between the two men over a number of issues, including the fate of the income obtained by the king from the Canterbury see during the vacancy; how to deal with immoral practices amongst the clergy; and which of the two popes (Urban II and Clement III) who had been elected to succeed Gregory VII should be recognized as legitimate. On this last issue, Anselm acknowledged Urban II, whereas William remained largely neutral but lent towards Clement III. The king apparently declared of Anselm that 'yesterday I hated him with great hatred, today I hate him with yet greater hatred and he can be certain that tomorrow and thereafter I shall hate him continually with ever fiercer and more bitter hatred.' A council convened at Rockingham (Northamptonshire) in 1095 was unable to effect a reconciliation. Anselm departed from England in 1097, only returning upon the death of William in 1100. By that time a number of bishoprics and abbacies had been left deliberately vacant by William.

Questions

1) Study Sources A–C. What reasons do these sources give for judging William II as being 'odious to God'?

2) 'The history of the actions of William II will never be properly known because those who recorded his actions were his enemies.' How far do you agree with this statement? Explain your answer.

Source A. Eadmer, *The History of Modern Times in England*. Eadmer was born around 1060. At least one of his parents was English. He grew up in the monastery of Christ Church in Canterbury and became a monk in that place. He was a regular companion of Anselm, travelling into exile with him. Eadmer died in about 1144.

> William II attacked the church of Canterbury. He ordered a list of their property to be drawn up by his officials. After fixing an allowance for the monks who served God there he put up the church of Christ for sale, granting the power of lordship over it to the highest bidder, no matter how great the damage incurred thereby. What scandals, discords and irregularities arose from this it pains me to record. Nor were such deeds confined to Canterbury. The same barbarity raged in every diocese in England. This king was the first to bring this baleful oppression against the Church of God he alone, when churches fell vacant, kept them in his own hands.

Source B. *Anglo-Saxon Chronicle*. The *Chronicle* was first begun at the end of the ninth century. It is a contemporary record of events, written by monks in England.

> 1100. [William II] was very strong and fierce to his country and his men and all his neighbours, and very terrible. In his days all justice was forgotten, and all injustice arose both in ecclesiastical [church] and secular matters. He abused God's Church, and all the bishoprics and abbacies whose incumbents [office holders] died in his days he sold for money or kept in his own hands and let out for rent. And so, on the day he died he had in his own hands the archbishopric of Canterbury, and the bishopric of Winchester and that of Salisbury, and eleven abbacies all let out for rent. All that was hateful to God and just men was all customary in this country in his time. [He was thus] odious to God.

Source C. William of Malmesbury, The *History of Recent Events* written 1140–42. William's father was Norman, and his mother was English. He spent his adult life as a monk in Malmesbury Abbey in England.

> I remember no council being held in [William II's] time wherein the health of the Church might have been strengthened by the correction of abuses. He delayed long in appointing to ecclesiastical offices, either for the sake of the money he gained thereby, or because he wished to consider the merits of those who might be advanced. Thus on the day he died he held in his own hands three vacant bishoprics, and twelve vacant abbeys.

8) Exam practice and online resources

Questions in the style of Edexcel

a) 4 marks per question

  i) Describe two features of a diocese.

 ii) Describe two features of monasticism.

iii) Describe two rulings of the *Dictatus Papae*

b) 12 marks per question

  i) Explain why William was determined to 'Normanize' the church. You may use the following in your answer:

- bishops and abbots
- rebellions

You must also use information of your own.

ii) Explain why the appointment of Lanfranc was important in terms of William securing his authority in England. You may use the following in your answer:

- Stigand
- Gregory VII

You must also use information of your own.

c) 16 marks

  i) 'The main consequence of the appointment of Lanfranc as archbishop of Canterbury in 1070 was an increase in Norman control of England.' How far do you agree? You may use the following in your answer:

- Archbishop Stigand
- monasteries

You must also use information of your own.

Questions in the style of AQA

a) 8 marks

  i) Study Source A. How convincing is this interpretation of Lanfranc? Explain your answer using Interpretation A and your contextual knowledge.

Source A. An Account of Lanfranc by H. E. J. Cowdrey in the *Oxford Dictionary of National Biography* (adapted).

A man of tireless and well-directed energy, to the end of his life he adapted himself confidently to the needs of each change in his circumstances. The relationship which, after 1072, he achieved with William I, a master of commanding ability whom he understood and respected, enabled him to leave English church and society far stronger than he found them after the traumas of the Conquest.

b) 8 marks per question

i) Explain why William 'Normanized' the church.

ii) Explain why the appointment of Lanfranc was important in terms of William securing his authority over England.

iii) Explain why relations between church and state deteriorated after the death of William I.

c) 8 marks per question

i) Write an account of Lanfranc's reforming councils.

ii) Write an account of why the pontificate of Gregory VII posed a threat to the authority of William I.

Online Resources

Take a look inside Selby Abbey http://www.simon-bowen.com/panoramas/selbyabbey/selbyAbbeyPano2.htm.

A virtual tour of Canterbury Cathedral http://www.canterbury-cathedral.org/visit/tour/.

8 THE DEATH OF WILLIAM THE CONQUEROR AND HIS LEGACY

Key Issues

Overview

This chapter examines the nature of the death of William the Conqueror. It relates what happened at his funeral and introduces the debate that surrounds his legacy. Some historians argue that 1066 represents a turning point in English history because William's policies were so different and restrictive that they created shackles on many people known as the 'Norman Yoke'. (A yoke is a wooden beam normally used between a pair of oxen or other animals to enable them to pull together on a load when working in pairs.) In contrast, other historians dismiss the notion of a 'Norman Yoke' and argue instead that continuity is more evident than change. These competing interpretations exist in part because the existing evidence often permits more than one interpretation. This chapter will help you to decide where you stand on the question of the impact of the arrival of the Normans.

1) How did William the Conqueror die and what happened at his funeral?

By the time of his death in 1087 William the Conqueror was in his late fifties and had grown fat, an uncomfortable condition for a warrior who fought on horseback. During another military campaign in July in the French Vexin, a territory from which the French king was launching attacks upon Normandy, William was injured when his horse jumped a ditch, forcing the pommel of his saddle deep into his protruding stomach. This accident caused internal injuries that hastened his demise. He was taken to the church of St Gervase, outside Rouen, and died there on 9 September.

Panic immediately ensued: some of the attendants mounted their horses and departed in haste to secure their properties; the remainder took whatever they considered to have any value, even the robes which William was wearing, leaving the corpse almost naked on the floor. Shortly afterwards the body was removed to Caen and buried in the abbey church of St Etienne, though, according to Orderic Vitalis, not without incident (see Source A, below).

William's grave has been disturbed on several occasions since 1087. The first time was in 1552, when the grave was opened on orders of the pope. In this instance the body was reinterred, but during the French Wars of Religion in the sixteenth century the grave was reopened. On this occasion the bones were scattered and lost – except for one thigh bone. This singular relic was reburied in 1642, though one eminent historian believes that this too was lost during the French Revolution.

Question

1) Study Sources A and B. To what extent has the author of Source B made use of Source A in his account of the funeral of William I? Explain your answer.

Source A. *The Ecclesiastical History* by Orderic Vitalis (1075–1142). Vitalis wrote his *History* between 1123 and 1141. He was born in England to a Norman father and an English mother.

> When the corpse was lowered into the stone coffin [the attendants] were obliged to use some violence in forcing it in, because through the negligence of the masons it had been made too short, so that, as the king was very corpulent, the bowels burst, and an intolerable stench affected the by-standers and the rest of the crowd. The smoke of incense and other aromatics ascended in clouds, but failed to purify the tainted atmosphere. The priests therefore hurried the conclusion of the funeral service and retired as soon as possible, in great alarm, to their respective abodes. I have thus carefully investigated, and given a true account of all the manifestations of God's providence (i.e. God's will) at the duke's death, not composing an imagined tragedy in order to earn money, nor a humorous comedy to provoke the laughter of parasites, but a true narrative of the various events for the perusal of studious readers.

Source B. Marc Morris, *The Norman Conquest* (2013).

> The greatest indignity was reserved until last. When William was finally lowered into the ground, it became clear that his bloated corpse was too big for its stone sarcophagus, and efforts to press on regardless caused his swollen bowels to burst. No amount of frankincense and spices could hide the resultant stench, and the clergy therefore raced through the rest of the funeral rite [ceremony] before rushing back to their houses.

2) What is understood by the term the 'Norman Yoke'?

Orderic Vitalis (1075–1142) alleged that from 1066 'the English groaned aloud for their lost liberty and plotted ceaselessly to find some way of shaking off a yoke that was so intolerable and unaccustomed'.

The notion that after 1066 the English were placed in shackles and oppressed in new ways and to a new extent is partly based on the widespread substitution of Normans for English amongst the ruling elite, both in secular and church offices. Domesday Book documents the extensive transfer of the major secular estates from Anglo-Saxon to Norman and French lords after 1066, the result of William rewarding his followers and thereby making them 'stakeholders' in the Conquest – ensuring that this was a change that was not going to be reversed. As Henry of Huntingdon (c.1088–c.1157) asserted, 'there was scarcely a noble of English descent in England, but all had been reduced to servitude [slavery] and lamentation' [unhappiness].

The transfer of land to the new ruling elite was accompanied by changes in the rules of landholding. The principle that all land was held from the king in return for certain services (usually military or religious service) was established, and, in addition, the nature of those services was tightened, and the tax liability of landholdings was clarified. New laws were introduced, such as the Forest Law (see p. 55) whose punishments were harsh to encourage compliance, and opposition to the Norman regime was suppressed ruthlessly.

The extent of these changes, and the presence of a new authority in England, was visibly reinforced through the construction of an ever-growing number of castles and the reconstruction of monumental cathedral churches. Many of these buildings were located in towns, that is, the administrative and military centres, and acted as symbols and instruments of power for the new Norman regime. The sounds in England were changing together with its sights. English ceased to be the language of court and administration, replaced by Latin, while the incomers spoke a form of French. The fact that William felt it necessary to introduce the *murdrum* fine (see Source D) strongly suggests resentment by the English of their new masters.

Source Investigation: the Norman Yoke. Study Sources A–E.

1) What evidence is there in these sources to support the idea of the 'Norman Yoke'?

2) Study Sources B and E. Which of these sources do you consider more reliable for a historian researching the nature of Norman rule? Explain your answer.

3) Study Source D. Some historians argue that this Source shows that William's rule was beneficial for the English; other historians have used

this Source to show that William's rule was detrimental for the English. Identify and explain how this Source carries two meanings.

Source A. *Anglo-Saxon Chronicle*, E. The *Chronicle* was first begun at the end of the ninth century. It is a contemporary record of events, written by monks in England.

1086–1087 [William] acted according to his custom – that is to say he obtained a very great amount of money wherever he had any reason for it whether just or otherwise. Earls he had in fetters [chains] – he expelled bishops from their sees, and abbots from their abbacies; he put thegns in prison and finally he did not spare his own brother, Odo.

Source B. *Anglo-Saxon Chronicle* E. (Very unusually, this particular entry of 1087 is made in verse.) The *Chronicle* was first begun at the end of the ninth century. It is a contemporary record of events, written by monks in England.

Certainly in his time people had much oppression and very many injuries.
He had castles built
And poor men hard oppressed
The king was so very stark
And deprived his underlings of many a mark
Of gold and more hundreds of pounds of silver
He made great protection for the game [hunting]
And imposed laws for the same
That who so slew hart or hind
Should be made blind
May Almighty God show mercy to his soul
And grant unto him forgiveness for his sins

Source C. Orderic Vitalis, *The Ecclesiastical History*. Vitalis (1075–1142) wrote his *History* between 1123 and 1141. He was born in England to a Norman father and an English mother. From about the age of ten he entered the monastery in Normandy, where he remained for the rest of his life. Here Orderic puts words into the mouth of William to create a deathbed speech.

I have persecuted the natives of England beyond all reason. Whether gentle or simple I have cruelly oppressed them; many I unjustly disinherited; innumerable multitudes perished through me by famine or the sword. Having gained the throne of that kingdom by so many crimes I dare not leave it to anyone but God.

Source D. From *The Laws of William the Conqueror* (This is the so-called *murdrum* fine.)

3. I command that all the men whom I have brought with me [from Normandy], or who have come after me, shall be protected by my peace and shall dwell in quiet. And if any one of them shall be slain, let the lord of his murderer seize him within five days, if he can. If he cannot, let him begin

to pay me 46 marks of silver until he runs out of money. When his money is exhausted let the whole community in which the murder took place pay what remains.

10. I also forbid that anyone shall be slain or hanged for any fault. Instead, let his eyes be put out and let him be castrated. And this command shall not be violated under pain of a fine in full to me.

Source E. William of Malmesbury, *The Modern History*, written 1140–42. William's father was Norman and his mother was English. He spent his adult life as a monk in Malmesbury abbey in England.

Normans and English, incited by different motives, have written about king William: the former have praised him to excess while the latter, out of national hatred, have laden their conqueror with undeserved reproach. For my part, as the blood of either people flows in my veins, I shall steer a middle course – where I am certain of his good deeds I shall openly proclaim them; his bad conduct I shall touch upon lightly nor will I brand [William] with harsh words, almost the whole of whose actions may reasonably be excused, if not condemned. [The occasion of the Battle of Hastings] was a fatal day for England, a melancholy havoc of our dear country brought about by its passing under the domination of new lords.

3) Did the 'Norman Yoke' exist?

The idea of a 'Norman Yoke' has been an enduring theme throughout English history. One explanation is that it has been a convenient construct for various groups resisting authority who wanted to present themselves as freedom fighters, such as the opponents of Charles I in the seventeenth century and those in the nineteenth century seeking to diminish the influence of the pope. It also draws upon the evidence (discussed in Chapters 5 and 6) of resistance to William, the changes he introduced and the anger of the dispossessed.

Yet other evidence exists which offers a different interpretation of the changes under William, and which downplays 1066 as a major 'turning point', and therefore casts doubt on the notion of a 'Norman Yoke'. William certainly tightened the terms and conditions of landholding, but he was essentially modifying an existing system, not creating a new one: the basic elements of 'feudalism' existed prior to 1066, and the Norman reform of English feudalism continued well into the twelfth century.

The new Norman king continued to govern England using many of the mechanisms, procedures and processes of Anglo-Saxon government. William issued writs that were the same in form and function – if not language (at least after the first few years following 1066) – as those issued by his predecessors. The system of taxation and coinage did not change. Although the new Norman landlords rearranged some manors and redefined the labour services owed by the existing Anglo-Saxon peasants, relations between them were mainly regulated by custom which protected the peasantry against major changes.

Norman influence was already established in England before 1066 – Edward the Confessor spent many years in Normandy, and some Normans held important positions within the church – and the process of assimilation accelerated immediately after 1066. There was rapid and extensive intermarriage between the English and Normans, and people at all levels of society began to choose Norman forenames in preference to Anglo-Saxon names. The single most commonly recorded name in the twelfth century was 'William'.

Some aspects of English life benefited from the arrival of the Normans. The number of slaves declined (though these people were recategorized as unfree peasants) and the practice spread of accepting money instead of labour services, both of which helped improve their standing and welfare. 'In this respect', wrote Lawrence of Durham (d. 1154), '[the English] found the foreigners treated them better than they had treated themselves'. The Norman concept of knighthood involved the introduction of codes of behaviour, including stopping the English practice of killing opponents after they had surrendered. Disloyal noblemen were more likely to be stripped of lands or fined than executed: after the execution of Earl Waltheof in 1076 no earl was similarly treated until the early fourteenth century. The Normans also contributed significantly to a religious revival. 'You could watch the country flourishing with renewed religious observance', noted William of Malmesbury (c.1095–c.1143).

4) Historical interpretations – was 1066 a 'turning point'?

Questions

1) Study Sources A–G.

For each source identify which one (or more) of these three historical interpretations is supported by the author:

   i) 1066 represents a 'turning point'

   ii) 1066 does not represent a 'turning point'

   iii) 1066 represents a 'turning point' in some ways but not in others

2) Why do you think historians are not able to agree about the nature of 1066 as a 'turning point'? Explain your answer.

3) If you were able to choose only one of Sources A–G to illustrate best your own view of the significance of 1066, which one would you choose? Explain your answer.

Source A. E. A. Freeman, *William the Conqueror* (1888).

> William founded no new state, no new nation, no new constitution; he simply kept what he found, with such modifications as his position made needful. But without any formal change in the nature of English kingship, his position enabled him to clothe the crown with a practical power such as it had never held before, to make his rule, in short, a virtual despotism [tyranny]. These two facts determined the later course of English history, and they determined it to the lasting good of the English nation. The conservative instincts of William allowed our national life and our national institutions to live on unbroken through his conquest.

Source B. William Stubbs, *Constitutional History of England* (1875).

> The effect of the Norman Conquest on the character and constitution of the English was threefold. The Norman rule invigorated the whole national system; it stimulated the growth of freedom and the sense of unity; and it supplied, partly from its own stock of jurisprudence [body of law], and partly under the pressure of the circumstances in which the conquerors found themselves, a formative power which helped develop and concentrate the wasted energies of the native race.

Source C. Pauline Stafford, *Women and the Norman Conquest* (1993).

Anglo-Saxon England has been seen as a Golden Age of women's legal emancipation, women's education and women's sexual liberation. A cursory view of a range of evidence from either side of the 1066 divide casts immediate doubt on the idea of a brutal Norman ending of the Golden Age. The raw statistics of Domesday, for example, suggest a different picture of England on the eve of the Norman arrival. No more than five per cent of the total hidage of land recorded was in the hands of women in 1066. Of that five per cent, 80–85% was in the hands of only eight women, almost all of them members of the families of the great earls, particularly of earl Godwin, or of the royal family. By the tenth and eleventh centuries women other than the queen are virtually absent from the witness lists of the royal charters, and thus apparently from the political significance such witness lists record. By contrast Norman and Anglo-Norman women strike [are noticeable] by the range and prominence of their activity. [For instance, twelfth-century Anglo-Norman charters regularly record the consent of wives, of mothers and sometimes even of daughters to land grants.] This evidence sits ill with [the argument that] 1066 and the coming of the Normans heralds a decline in women's status.

Source D. David Bates, *William the Conqueror* (1989).

It can be argued that the Conquest was not a process of change which was confined to William's reign, since the Normans continued to arrive in England until well into the twelfth century and major changes continued to take place. [Even if the effects and consequences of the Conquest are limited to William's reign] the results are extraordinarily diverse. There is, for example, massive variation from one region to another – for instance, ports in southern England benefitted from increased contact with the Continent whereas areas of northern England suffered an economic and social catastrophe.

Source E. D. C. Douglas, *William the Conqueror* (1964).

The Norman conquest of England was perhaps the most revolutionary event in English history between the Conversion [to Christianity] and the Reformation. It gave to England a new monarchy, a feudal polity [regime] of a special type, a reconstituted Church, and a changed concentration on a new set of political and intellectual ideas. But at the same time, it was so achieved as to ensure the essential continuity of English life. By combining much that was new with the revival of much that was old, it went far to determine the highly individual character of England.

Source F. R. Allen Brown, *The Normans and the Norman Conquest* (1985).

[Perhaps] the two most profound results of the Norman Conquest, which between them set the pattern of future English history, [were] a far closer association with the Continent than before (particularly the breaking of existing ties with Scandinavia and their replacement by stronger bonds with northern France) … [and the development] of the unity of England. On the basis of this unity the lines of future expansion were marked out [into Ireland, Scotland and Wales.]

5) Exam questions and online resources

Questions in the style of Edexcel

a) 4 marks

i) Describe two features of the 'Norman Yoke'

b) 16 marks

i) 'It is historically mistaken to argue that 1066 represents a "turning point" in English history'. How far do you agree? You may use the following in your answer:

- the circumstances of women
- changes in landholding

You must also use information of your own.

Questions in the style of AQA

a) 8 marks

i) Study Source A. How convincing is this interpretation of the impact of the Norman Conquest of 1066? Explain your answer using Interpretation A and your contextual knowledge.

Source A. Frank Barlow, *The Feudal Kingdom of England 1042–1216* (1955).

> William's struggle to keep his throne and the successful breaking of all resistance transformed the power of the English monarchy, and led to changes in the composition of the nobility and of the high clergy, and governmental method, and in the arrangement of society. After William had reigned for twenty years, the result of the Battle of Hastings had become not simply the substitution of William for Harold as King, but the intrusion of the Norman way of life into many spheres of activity.

b) 8 marks per question

i) Explain the concept of the 'Norman Yoke'.

ii) Explain why the concept of the 'Norman Yoke' has been criticized.

c) 8 marks

i) Write an account of the ways in which the impact of the Norman Conquest has been variously interpreted.

Online Resources

An essay by Michael Wood – 'The "Norman Yoke": Symbol or Reality?' http://www.bbc.co.uk/history/trail/conquest/after_norman/norman_yoke_01.shtml.

BBC Radio 4 In Our Time. Melvyn Bragg and guests discuss the 'Norman Yoke' http://www.bbc.co.uk/programmes/b009q7zm.

Glossary

abbot: Head of a monastery.

aetheling: A title given to a son of the king, meaning 'throne worthy'.

amercement: Monetary fine.

Ancient Demesne: Personal lands and estates of the king, in the sense that they passed from king to king in succession, and their purpose was to support the king's household and the expenses.

Anglo-Saxon: People from Germanic tribes – principally the Angles, Saxons and Jutes – who migrated to England from the fifth century.

archbishop: A leading bishop, of whom there were two – one whose church was at Canterbury; the other whose church was at York.

bishop: A member of the clergy who presided in a church housing a cathedra, a Latin word meaning seat or throne.

blood feud: A system whereby a murdered person's family could legitimately seek out and kill the murderer.

borough: A town.

burgesses: A freeman of a borough.

burhs: Fortified settlements.

Chancery: Department of royal government that administered writs and charters.

charter: A royal instruction bestowing a grant of privileges or rights to an individual or group of recipients, usually over land.

Christianity: Belief that Jesus is the Son of God and the Messiah.

church: A reference to the administrative organization of the institutions and offices that deliver Christianity.

clergy: Members of the church, for example, priests and bishops.

coronation: A ceremony undertaken formally to assume the office of king. In front of the bishops the king took a threefold oath: to preserve the peace of the church and the Christian people; to prohibit looting and crime; and to maintain justice. The king was then anointed with holy oil, usually by the archbishop of Canterbury. After that the king was presented with a sword with which to defend the church and to protect the weak; a crown was placed upon his head; and finally he was presented with an orb and sceptre (a rod), the former representing Christ's supremacy over the world and the latter indicating the king's authority over all other laymen.

Danegeld: A national tax first raised in 991 used to buy peace from the Danes.

Danelaw: That part of England in which the laws of the Danes held sway.

demesne: Agricultural land belonging to a lord, used as a home farm to grow crops and rear livestock for the lord's benefit.

diocese or see: Territory governed by a bishop or archbishop.

ealdorman: An official who exercised jurisdiction (command) on the king's behalf over a wide swathe of territory, called an earldom, and was responsible for acting in the king's name in areas where the king himself could not regularly visit to provide personal rule. The title evolved to that of earl.

earl: See ealdorman.

earldom: Territory presided over by an earl.

episcopacy: Government of the church by bishops.

excommunication: The action of officially excluding someone from participation in the sacraments (e.g. the Mass) and services of the Christian Church.

fealty: See homage.

fief: A number of manors.

forfeiture: Loss of land suffered by a vassal if he failed to fulfil the terms of the grant, for example, military service.

freemen: Men who could leave their village, and transfer their land to other people, without their lord's permission.

fyrd: Locally raised militia, a fighting force.

harrying: Undertaking acts of destruction.

Heptarchy: Collective name referencing the seven Anglo-Saxon kingdoms: Northumbria; Merica; East Anglia; Essex; Kent; Sussex; and Wessex.

Hidage: Every five hides had to provide one warrior for the army.

hide: A hide was a unit of taxation, based on an area of cultivated land roughly equivalent to perhaps 120 acres, though recent research has indicated that it in fact had a very variable extent on the ground.

hoard: Items of value, buried in the ground.

homage: The swearing of an oath of loyalty – 'fealty' – in return for the grant of land.

hundred: A territorial division of the shire.

huscarls: Originally known as thegns – see thegn.

knight's fee: A fief of sufficient size to support one fighting knight, that is, to pay for his equipment, horse and support.

magnate: A person of great influence and status; a leading nobleman.

manor: Basic territory unit of lordship, comprising arable land, pasture, houses, woodland and other economic resources, such as fisheries, mills and mineral rights.

minority: A period when a monarch is not yet of a sufficient age to govern in their own right.

outlaw: A title given to someone who did not attend court, meaning that they could be killed by anyone without the perpetrator receiving punishment.

papacy: Office held by the pope as head of the Roman Catholic Church.

pagan: Someone who held a religious belief other than Christianity.

parish: A territorial unit constituting a division within a diocese; each parish possessed a church.

reeve: A local official.

regent: A person who possesses the authority of the king / queen when the king / queen is incapacitated from governing, for instance because of age or illness.

Romanesque: A style of architecture associated especially with the Normans.

royal forest: Land that was subject to a specific body of laws, known as forest law.

sheriff: The king's chief executive agent in every branch of local government.

shire: An area of territory, the equivalent of the modern county.

shire reeve: See sheriff.

sub-infeudation: The process of granting manors as fiefs below the level of tenants-in-chief.

tenants-in-chief: Lords who held their land directly from the king.

thegns: Originally the personal bodyguards of the king, but latterly lords of local importance who were prominent in the localities.

tithe: A payment made to the church, amounting to one-tenth of the harvest or stock.

tithings: System by which local communities were held responsible for maintaining law and order by 'pushing' cases of wrongdoing to court.

vassal: Term describing a person granted a fief/manor by a superior lord.

virgate: Unit of land usually reckoned as one-fourth of a hide, equal to 30 acres.

wergild: A system of fines as compensation for breaches of the law.

witenagemot/witan: A meeting of the king with the leading members of the aristocracy to discuss key matters of state.

woad: A plant used as a source of blue dye.

writ: A royal instruction, written down, to a named individual or group of recipients.

Acknowledgements

Every effort has been made to identify the authors of sources used in this book. If an acknowledgement is missing please contact the publishers so that this can be amended.

Chapter 1

p. 3 Based on Jones and Mattingley's *Atlas of Roman Britain*, 1990. Credit: ©Jon Williams; **p. 3** Credit: © The Trustees of the British Museum; **p. 6** Based on Martin Gilbert, *The Dent Atlas of British History*, Dent, 1993. Credit: © Jon Williams; **p. 6** transl by W. A. McDevitte and W. S. Bohn, 1869; **p. 7** Credit: © Jon Williams; **p. 9** Based on Jones & Mattingly's *Atlas of Roman Britain*. Credit: © Jon Williams; **p. 9** The translation is from: *Six Old English Chronicles*. Ed. J. A. Giles. London: Henry G. Bohn, 1848; **p. 10** Source: The Venerable Bede, *Bede's Ecclesiastical History of England* trans. and ed. A. M. Sellar (London: George Bell, 1907), 28–31; **p. 11** Credit: © Jon Williams; **p. 12** Reproduced with permission from BBC, http://www.bbc.co.uk/history/ancient/british_prehistory/peoples_01.shtml; **14** Credit: © Jon Williams; **p. 15** Based on a map in Hill, *An Atlas of Anglo-Saxon England*. Credit: © Jon Williams; **p. 15** Chris Heaton. Source: Chris Heaton; **p. 16** Source: David Hemming; **p. 17** Credit: © Jon Williams; **p. 18** Source: Archiwum Własne Wikingów; **p. 19** Credit: © Jon Williams; **p. 20** Credit: © Jon Williams; **p. 21** Credit: © Jon Williams; **p. 22** From *English Historical Documents 500–1042*, Volume 1, edited by Dorothy Whitelock, © 1955 Routledge, reproduced by permission of Taylor & Francis Books, UK; **p. 22** From F. Barlow, *Edward the Confessor*, California Press, 1970 p. 3; **p. 22** From *English Historical Documents 500–1042*, Volume 1, edited by Dorothy Whitelock, © 1955 Routledge, reproduced by permission of Taylor & Francis Books, UK; **p. 24** Credit: Image courtesy of York Museums Trust; **p. 25** From *English Historical Documents 500–1042*, Volume 1, edited by Dorothy Whitelock, © 1955 Routledge, reproduced by permission of Taylor & Francis Books, UK; **p. 27** Credit: © Jon Williams; **p. 29** Source: Kernot Geller;

p. 30 Source: Sutton Hoo helmet. (http://projects.oucs.ox.ac.uk/woruldhord/) by Ian Harvey, licensed as Creative Commons BY-NC-SA (2.0 UK); **p. 32** Credit: Reproduced by kind permission of the Syndics of Cambridge University Library (http://cudl.lib.cam.ac.uk/view/MS-EE-00003-00059/23); **p. 34** Credit: © Jon Williams; **p. 35** Based on *An Atlas of Anglo-Saxon England* by David Hill. Credit: © Jon Williams; **p. 37** Based on *An Atlas of Anglo-Saxon England* by David Hill. Credit: © Jon Williams; **p. 37** Credit: © Jon Williams; **p. 39** Reproduced with permission from the Bodleian Libraries, University of Oxford, MS. Junius 11, page 57 (detail); **p. 40** Credit: © Jon Williams; **p. 42** Credit: © Jon Williams; **p. 44** Credit: © Jon Williams; **p. 45** Every effort has been made to trace copyright holders and to obtain their permission to reproduce this material; any further information related to the rightsholder if notified will be incorporated in future reprints or editions of this book;

Chapter 2

p. 52 From *English Historical Documents 500–1042*, Volume 1, edited by Dorothy Whitelock, © 1955 Routledge, reproduced by permission of Taylor & Francis Books, UK; **p. 53** Credit: © Jon Williams; **p. 53** Credit: Reproduced with permission from The National Archives, ref. KB26/223; **p. 55** Credit: © Jon Williams; **p. 56** From *English Historical Documents 1042–1189*, Volume 1, edited by David Douglas and George Greenaway, © 1953 Routledge, reproduced by permission of Taylor & Francis Books, UK; **p. 58** Credit: © Jon Williams; **p. 61** Credit: © Jon Williams; **p. 62** Copyright © The British Library Board (http://www.bl.uk/onlinegallery/ttp/luttrell/accessible/pages21and22.html#content)**65** Credit: © Jon Williams; **p. 66** From *English Historical Documents*

1042–1189, Volume 1, edited by David Douglas and George Greenaway, © 1953 Routledge, reproduced by permission of Taylor & Francis Books, UK; **p. 67** © Alecto Historical Editions 1986; **p. 68** Credit: © Jon Williams; **p. 69** Credit: © Jon Williams; **p. 70** From *English Historical Documents 1042–1189*, Volume 1, edited by David Douglas and George Greenaway, © 1953 Routledge, reproduced by permission of Taylor & Francis Books, UK; **p. 00** From *English Historical Documents 1042–1189*, Volume 1, edited by David Douglas and George Greenaway, © 1953 Routledge, reproduced by permission of Taylor & Francis Books, UK; **p. 73** Credit: Reproduced with permission of The National Archives; **p. 00** By permission of Oxford University Press (URL www.oup.com); **p. 75** From *Ruling England 1042–1217* by R. Huscroft p. 38, Routledge, with permission;

Chapter 3

p. 79 Credit: © Jon Williams; **p. 81** Credit: © Jon Williams; **p. 81** From *English Historical Documents 1042–1189*, Volume 1, edited by David Douglas and George Greenaway, © 1953 Routledge, reproduced by permission of Taylor & Francis Books, UK; **p. 82** Source: https://epistolae.ccnmtl. columbia.edu/letter/52.html; **p. 84** Credit: © Jon Williams; **p. 86** From *English Historical Documents 1042–1189*, Volume 1, edited by David Douglas and George Greenaway, © 1953 Routledge, reproduced by permission of Taylor & Francis Books, UK; **p. 87** Credit: From 'Life of St Edward the Confessor (MS Ee.3.59)', http://cudl.lib.cam.ac.uk/view/MS-EE-00003-00059/54; **p. 89** Source: Author's translation of the script in Barlow's *The Life of King Edward*; **p. 90** Credit: © Jon Williams; **p. 91** Credit: © Jon Williams; **p. 92** Credit: © Jon Williams; **p. 93** From English Historical Documents 1042–1189, Volume 1, edited by David Douglas and George Greenaway, © 1953 Routledge, reproduced by permission of Taylor & Francis Books, UK; **p. 93** From English Historical Documents 1042–1189, Volume 1, edited by David Douglas and George Greenaway, © 1953 Routledge, reproduced by permission of Taylor & Francis Books, UK; **p. 94** From English Historical Documents 1042–1189, Volume 1, edited by David Douglas and George Greenaway, © 1953 Routledge, reproduced by permission of Taylor & Francis Books, UK; **p. 94** Credit: © Jon Williams; **p. 95** Reproduced with permission of UC Press; Every effort has been

made to trace copyright holders and to obtain their permission to reproduce this material; any further information related to the rightsholders if notified will be incorporated in future reprints or editions of this book; **p. 97** From English Historical Documents 1042–1189, Volume 1, edited by David Douglas and George Greenaway, © 1953 Routledge, reproduced by permission of Taylor & Francis Books, UK; **p. 98** Credit: © Jon Williams; **p. 100** Source: Cambridge University Library, http://cudl.lib.cam.ac.uk/view/MS-EE-00003-00059/54**100** Credit: © Jon Williams; **p. 101** Credit: Reproduced with permission of Bloomsbury, Osprey publishing; **p. 103** Every effort has been made to trace copyright holders and to obtain their permission to reproduce this material; any further information related to the rightsholder if notified will be incorporated in future reprints or editions of this book; **p. 103** Credit: © Jon Williams; **p. 104** Credit: Birney Lettick/National Geographic Creative;

Chapter 4

p. 107 Credit: ©Jon Williams'; **p. 107** From *English Historical Documents 1042–1189*, Volume 1, edited by David Douglas and George Greenaway, © 1953 Routledge, reproduced by permission of Taylor & Francis Books, UK; **p. 108** From *English Historical Documents 1042–1189*, Volume 1, edited by David Douglas and George Greenaway, © 1953 Routledge, reproduced by permission of Taylor & Francis Books, UK; **p. 110** Credit: ©Jon Williams; **p. 111** Every effort has been made to trace copyright holders and to obtain their permission to reproduce this material; any further information related to the rightsholder if notified will be incorporated in future reprints or editions of this book; **p. 115** Credit: © Jon Williams; **p. 117** Credit: Tom Lovell/National Geographic Creative; **p. 118** From *English Historical Documents 1042–1189*, Volume 1, edited by David Douglas and George Greenaway, © 1953 Routledge, reproduced by permission of Taylor & Francis Books, UK; **p. 118** Credit: ©Jon Williams; **p. 119** Extract (c.65w) from The Carmen de Hastingae Proelio of Guy, Bishop of Amiens, edited and translated by Frank Barlow (1999). By permission of Oxford University Press; **p. 119** From *English Historical Documents 1042–1189*, Volume 1, edited by David Douglas and George Greenaway, © 1953 Routledge, reproduced by permission of

Taylor & Francis Books, UK; **p. 120** From *English Historical Documents 1042–1189*, Volume 1, edited by David Douglas and George Greenaway, © 1953 Routledge, reproduced by permission of Taylor & Francis Books, UK; **p. 120** From *English Historical Documents 1042–1189*, Volume 1, edited by David Douglas and George Greenaway, © 1953 Routledge, reproduced by permission of Taylor & Francis Books, UK; **p. 120** From *English Historical Documents* 1042–1189, Volume 1, edited by David Douglas and George Greenaway, © 1953 Routledge, reproduced by permission of Taylor & Francis Books, UK; **p. 122** Credit: ©Jon Williams; **p. 123** From *English Historical Documents 1042–1189*, Volume 1, edited by David Douglas and George Greenaway, © 1953 Routledge, reproduced by permission of Taylor & Francis Books, UK; **p. 124** Source: Northallerton Hospital; **p. 125** Credit: © Jon Williams; **p. 127** Credit: Birney Lettick/National Geographic Creative;

Chapter 5

p. 131 From *English Historical Documents 1042–1189*, Volume 1, edited by David Douglas and George Greenaway, © 1953 Routledge, reproduced by permission of Taylor & Francis Books, UK; **p. 131** Extract (c.160w) from *The Ecclesiastical History of Orderic Vitalis*, Volume 2: Books 3 and 4, edited and translated by Marjorie Chibnall (1990). By permission of Oxford University Press, Inc; **p. 132** Extract (c.100w) p.217 from *The Ecclesiastical History of Orderic Vitalis*, Volume 4, edited and translated by Marjorie Chibnall (1968). By permission of Oxford University Press, Inc; **p. 133** Credit: © Jon Williams; **p. 137** Credit: ©Jon Williams; **p. 138** Reproduced with permission of UC Press. Every effort has been made to trace copyright holders and to obtain their permission to reproduce this material; any further information related to the rightsholders if notified will be incorporated in future reprints or editions of this book; **p. 141** Credit: © Jon Williams; **p. 142** Credit: © Jon Williams; **p. 142** Credit: © Jon Williams; **p. 143** From *English Historical Documents 1042–1189*, Volume 1, edited by David Douglas and George Greenaway, © 1953 Routledge, reproduced by permission of Taylor & Francis Books, UK; **p. 143** From *English Historical Documents 1042–1189*, Volume 1, edited by David Douglas and George Greenaway, © 1953 Routledge, reproduced by permission of Taylor & Francis Books, UK; **p. 143** Credit: © Graham Seel; **p. 147** Credit: © Jon Williams; **p. 148** Every effort has been made to trace copyright holders and to obtain their permission to reproduce this material; any further information related to the rightsholder if notified will be incorporated in future reprints or editions of this book; **p. 149** From *The Normans and the Norman Conquest*, R. Allen Brown 1969, 2000, Boydell Press. Reprinted by permission of Boydell & Brewer Ltd; **p. 152** Extract (c.100w) p. 217 from *The Ecclesiastical History of Orderic Vitalis*, Volume 4, edited and translated by Marjorie Chibnall (1968). By permission of Oxford University Press, Inc; **p. 152** Reproduced with permission of UC Press. Every effort has been made to trace copyright holders and to obtain their permission to reproduce this material; any further information related to the rightsholders if notified will be incorporated in future reprints or editions of this book; **p. 154** Credit: © Jon Williams. © Historic England Archive; **p. 155** Credit: Look and Learn; **p. 156** *The Medieval Castle in England and Wales* by N. J. G. Pounds. Reproduced by permission of Cambridge University Press;

Chapter 6

p. 161 Credit: © Jon Williams; **p. 162** From *English Historical Documents 1042–1189*, Volume 1, edited by David Douglas and George Greenaway, © 1953 Routledge, reproduced by permission of Taylor & Francis Books, UK; **p. 163** Extract (c. 300w) p. 315 from *The Ecclesiastical History of Orderic Vitalis*, Volume 2, edited and translated by Marjorie Chibnall (1969). By permission of Oxford University Press, Inc; **p. 168** From *English Historical Documents 1042–1189*, Volume 1, edited by David Douglas and George Greenaway, © 1953 Routledge, reproduced by permission of Taylor & Francis Books, UK; **p. 168** Credit: Look and Learn; **p. 169** Every effort has been made to trace copyright holders and to obtain their permission to reproduce this material; any further information related to the rightsholder if notified will be incorporated in future reprints or editions of this book; **p. 171** Credit: © Jon Williams; **p. 172** Credit: Look and Learn; **p. 173** From *English Historical Documents 1042–1189*, Volume 1, edited by David Douglas and

Index

Lightning Source UK Ltd.
Milton Keynes UK
UKHW031100281118
333109UK00003B/45/P